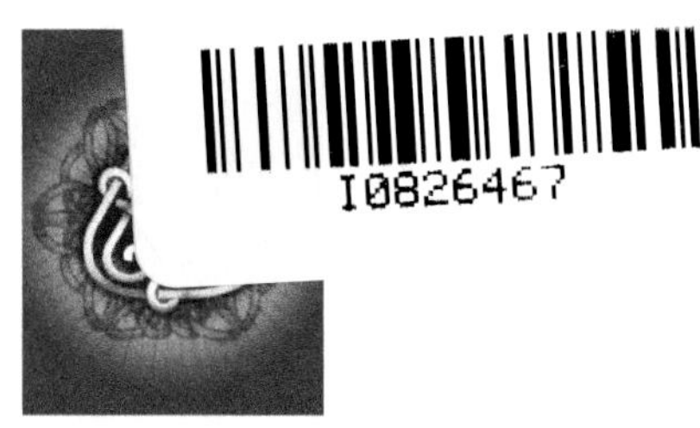

This book is dedicated to all of my Irish ancestors and incredible family both here and seemingly not here.

Living the Spiral ™

Registered ISBN 978-0-9800058-0-6

Cover photograph Glencar Falls, Ireland

For information on upcoming **Living the Spiral** or other Spa Resort events, or appts with Cathleen Miller please see

www.livingthespiral.com

Nature Spirit Publishing, US

Living the Spiral

Introduction

The ancient labyrinth has been used for centuries in countless sacred rituals to help initiate new beginnings for many cultures around the world. Many went reverently to the labyrinth in prayer to heal the physical body. Some went ready to break free from personal challenges, or addictions blocking their growth. Others held a focus to initiate their mind and soul into greater possibilities. All of these clearings and more can be accomplished through this program, as you learn to access your own inner potential ready and waiting within this sacred symbol.

The labyrinth is an ancient tool that when properly utilized, creates an expansion of one's path direction through a network of passages, opening higher senses in the process. This peaks as one suddenly arrives at the center and can experience the core point of any elaborate labyrinth design. There are countless labyrinth styles dating back to the beginning of recorded history. In this program, we will use the modern version of the triple spiral labyrinth which is relatively simple, (1-30 day triple spiral process on back cover). The triple spiral is a powerful instrument serving as a template to help you create the shifts you are now ready to compose in your life.

One of the most famous destinations containing this triple spiral labyrinth (since there are so many variations), can still be seen today in Newgrange, Ireland. In ancient times many believed drawing these spirals around the home, over doors, or outside on the ground would bring protection and increase fertile blessings from the great divine mother. The spiral design is also symbolic of the triple spiral goddess Saint Brigit who is still honored today by an ongoing fire in Kildare, Ireland.

Living the Spiral is a divine opportunity for you to experience greater wellbeing than ever before. This book is a thirty day cleansing program spiraling you into your own unique adventure, found within your own core. In completing this whole self-cleanse you can improve your physical health, strengthen your mental clarity, refine your intuitive abilities and connect more spiritually. You can also fine tune your relationships, while increasing your connection to divine source to help better guide every aspect of your life.

Your journey is well outlined and mapped out with daily resources through each of the thirty days. Every day you will have affirmations, meditation points to consider, and daily personal questions for your own growth and process. The back cover is also a full color mini labyrinth finger chart to follow (even if only by your finger or cotton swab q-tip). You can follow along on this small colored labyrinth spiral as often you are guided to do so. Or you may choose to copy this spiral symbol into your own yard or home to support your own personal growth in the spiral process.

By following this month long adventure you get to experience being inside this labyrinth for yourself. Before entering, you must first send your intentions and goals about your own body, mind, and spirit into this sacred space. Once in the spiral, you can gain clarity and enough inner strength to be able to realize your own highest personal vision. I will point out the highlights in the terrain surrounding you, serving as your guide to help light the way. I hold light from source as your own light awakens and expands so you may help light others around you.

There are very simple ways to make your own labyrinth. I have included step by step practical instructions to keep your goals attainable (alongside the time constraints of a busy work and personal life). Building your own labyrinth can be as easy as using a stick in the dirt (or sand at the beach). Or as elaborate as you would like to get with whatever your imagination brings forth. You can use rocks, string, or plant swirls of flowers outside to recreate your own personal expression of this sacred symbol.

Please remember that your intention matters more than the form, or materials used. Even the miniature finger labyrinths coupled with strong intention to heal can still create remarkable changes for you. The triple spiral is a powerful instrument for your consciousness to open and expand from. Since this works on many levels simultaneously, it will help you to create shifts on a much deeper level. In healing your 'whole' energetic system on many different levels, you get to experience a multi-dimensional existence within this process. Doing this helps to further awaken your connection to every aspect of life around you, while helping you to find your place within that connection.

By now most of us have gone through some sort of restrictive diet in attempt to release toxins from our body. Often when we seek change in our life, there are efforts made without much conscious awareness. Often this can leave us with temporary results, if any at all. Or when we release destructive habits through prayer or meditation (without the physical follow through), our results can again be temporary.

Since completing this month long cycle myself, I have experienced a multitude of benefits. A few include better sleep, weight loss (physical), increased clairvoyance, more balanced energy and clarity throughout the day (mental). I have also recommitted to a deeper yoga practice and find more patience and compassion with everything (spiritual). I am maintaining better overall balance of my entire system and staying in a high conscious flow more than ever before. These examples illustrate just a few of the infinite improvements that you can also attain from your own commitment here.

Each day I share journaling from my own daily experience to help inspire you by sharing my own transformation, alongside yours. What I thought would be a fun adventure literally took on a life of its own each day because of the strength of this morphogenic field. The universe brought me people, events, and intuitive experiences that opened and expanded my entire being more than I ever imagined possible. As we open to the soul initiations of sacred ceremony within this spiral and our highest soul path will find us.

I have worked for over a decade now as a multi certified healer; professional artist, teacher, and intuitive counselor. My intuitive sound and body work help to release lower patterns that are keeping many off their own higher path, while aligning them more to their true nature. Life experiences gained from this work have equipped me with a rich background of tools, resources and knowledge. Therefore I feel I am a qualified expedition guide to lead you here in your own personal quest for higher good. Remember that as we do our part to meet up with the transformation potential within each spiral, miracles can and do happen at every turn. Allow the miracles that are seeking you.

Chapter One
Entering the spiral

While admiring the vibrant red hibiscus peeking out under the enormous bird of paradise palms, I smiled into the salty breeze rolling off the intercoastal. Continuing along my morning walk, I began to see full color snapshot visuals of this triple spiral symbol. I knew right away that this was an opportunity to chart out this process for others to heal and grow from. I spontaneously envisioned myself teaching groups in alternative healing retreat spa centers around the world. I saw people having incredible breakthroughs from this program everywhere. I knew some would be leaving harmful addictive lifestyle patterns behind so they could rebirth into higher potential in every way.

After seeing several layers of this labyrinth chart visually, I was guided to inscribe this as soon as possible after getting home from my walk. After intuitively drawing out this image in a swift pace, the process solidified into clearer focus. Staring back at me was a thirty day trek through specifically colored spiral loops representing each day through this process. I knew each of these colors corresponded to a daily chakra to be explored and cleared in different dimensional levels each day.

Now I understand why such an urgent pace surged forth with this process. It was so I would not think through this imprint of information and alter it from my own ego tinkering. I admit to not understanding this initially and even questioned its sequence several times, until I had completed the 30 day process myself. Now after my own achievement, I realize in hindsight that it was (of course) in divine order. That was the gift for me to gain through challenge of trust. For me, this built a deeper trust with the entire universe. Healing my own trust issues strengthened me through each experience that magically appeared daily as I was guided to follow each unique day.

If you look on the back cover you can see the triple spiral labyrinth has three multi-colored coils of equal size that all connect at a middle point. You will follow the spirals as they are marked numerically each day beginning on the pink colored day marked number one at the center of the spirals.

Each single spiral of the trinity is shows a separate circular phase of ten days each. The first spiral of the physical body starts on the pink day (marked #1) in the center of the whole design. This inner heart pink color goes up (or north) heading inbound from the core (or center of the body spiral) over the next five days. Follow the color swatches that change daily, as you swirl inwards in a clockwise direction to the center. Once at the center you will then continue outbound for the next 5 days, spiraling out to day ten. Following this pattern will proceed counter-clockwise in the same spiral for the next five days until you reach the outer ring of the final brown colored day ten.

Following this brown line leads you around the outside of the body spiral then working into day 11 of the mind spiral. You may notice an extra layer on the mind has a full loop of brown transition around it. I didn't even really notice this extra layer until I was done with the program myself. When I meditated about the meaning of this, I was shown this extra loop had special significance. Healing the mind takes a much greater transition, and can be more work than the body or spirit, which tend to both follow the lead of the mind. For most of us, a complete inner shift of the mind needs this extra loop of 'transition' support. Our body and spirit need less energy and work than the healing and enlightenment of the mind.

As you transition to the mind spiral, you will proceed east going clockwise around the outside of the second spiral from day ten winding into day fifteen. Day fifteen is the halfway point of the entire process and can be a powerful core pivotal point for many. You will then proceed out of the mind going counterclockwise from day sixteen to twenty. Here we transition again, heading into the final spiral phase of spirit beginning on day twenty.

In the final spiral of spirit, we head west repeating the same rhythm of five days going within to the core in a clockwise fashion. Then day twenty six you will move outward counter clockwise to reach the end on day thirty. The final day of green and pink together symbolize the activated balanced inner heart. This line encircles the entire labyrinth design (including every spiral) to celebrate the whole self being infused with higher divine love and alignment.

On day thirty this sacred ceremony ends within the heart chakra (where it began). Here you can illuminate and rebirth into a higher state of being. The final step is when you symbolically reemerge, as you consciously step over the ring (or symbol outline) back into the starting center point. The symbolism is to consciously step into your own clear center point where you can then experience your own greater potential as a newly refined whole self.

We all deserve to be free of our past. Free of old relationships, habits and addictions that have plagued many of us for far too long. At only a few weeks old, my doctor shrugged his shoulders on what to do about my chronic digestive challenges and allergies. Not sure how to communicate my unique energetic abilities from a young age, I coped by cycling from uncontrollable overeating to obsessively fit and health conscious. I then swung back and forth between the two lifestyles for many years. This pattern continued well into my early twenties until I finally broke the chronic chain of imbalance.

For over a decade I was in countless detox programs, while simultaneously engaging in ongoing alternative therapies. This was an attempt to excavate my own natural rhythm in life. I read everything I could get my hands on both nutritionally and therapeutically, studying habits and new modalities attempting to stop my own pendulum swing. I applied most everything I found often with mixed results. Through trial and error (and great expense) I eventually learned what really worked for me. I also discovered how to holistically maintain vibrant health. Soon I began to share this knowledge with others realizing I could intuitively direct others to find the resources they needed as well.

The healing power of the triple spiral holds the

potential to break ancient patterns we may all carry. Once free of these old chains we can potentially establish a higher level of balance and inner strength than we have ever known. For some this may be a release of just one addictive habit for the month. For others this month will be a true life overhaul of positive transformation. In working with hundreds of people with this Spiral program for several years now I have seen countless miracles from the work. We all benefit as we release the core hooks of many binding etherical tethers to free ourselves up for a lighter life experience. Whatever you apply through your own efforts here is where the universe will meet you. There is incredible super conscious support here to help you achieve your desired level of inner renovation.

Within this thirty day process I will share my own personal journal insights. As you intend to obtain a higher level of peace, healing, and self-love within your own mind, body and spirit, you set the universe in motion to achieve it. Together we can laugh, have fun, breathe, and share the greatest adventure ever. Cleansing can be work as we undo our old stubborn habits and detrimental short cut ways. Enjoy this sacred time and remember to love yourself gently through the process.

Anything is possible.

Packing for the trip

As you prepare for your journey, there are a few things to consider before you begin. Journaling your intentions and goals for this expedition will reveal and help clarify what you wish to accomplish. Your goals are very important to have written down as you begin this process. I have been guided to share my own experience about what has accelerated my own personal healing. No matter where you are in your own life, there is always another level of consciousness to reach. The question is how much we will allow ourselves to receive in terms of health, joy, financial flow, inner peace and so on.

If you have any health concerns or plan to enter this month long experience with any shifts to your diet or personal routine, please consult with your own physician first to find what level of dietary changes or detoxification are appropriate for you proceed with. Our bodies and constitutions are so individually unique and this really needs to be respected. Go at your own pace and trust the level of changes that feel right for you alongside sound guidance. If you are on any medication or seeking medical or mental health care of any kind, please seek professional guidance before making any personal changes to be sure this program is right and approved for you to begin.

For me personally I am going to use a thirty day cleansing kit which includes healing herbs, vibrational essences, and daily fiber. This will be in conjunction with a healing organic diet, daily meditation, exercise, and other guided activities which I will explain in detail as we continue forward. There are many great cleansing products out there. I encourage you to find the right one for your level of health and budget since these factors can vary greatly. You may be led to just make dietary changes and remove junk food which is fine. I have been cleansing off and on for over twenty years now, and use many different products depending on what I am working on. The resource page on my website www.livingthespiral.com can refer products that I have personally used and found beneficial. I only list what I have personally used and find to be of high quality and integrity.

For your own cleansing and budget you may just want to simply add a good quality fiber and simple cleansing herbs that you are drawn to from your own local health food store. See the **Resource Guide** at the end of the book for a huge section of recommendations that you can use throughout the month. Doing this will help keep you organized as you continue and keep your daily routine as simple as possible. Often times just releasing all forms of sugar, white flour, low quality oils, preservatives, and lower quality refined items alone will begin a cleansing affect in the body. Even adding a high quality fiber may be enough to start a mild cleansing shift in the body. Whether you are a beginner or a seasoned cleanser, going to a quality local health food store or community organic garden is the first stop. High quality organic markets or your own quality local health food store often carry items from high integrity companies. Here they can guide you to the right high quality cleansing products to meet your needs and budget.

As for diet choices on this cleanse, you must first consider where you are health wise at the moment. Then set your goals from this starting point considering your personal health and weight. Too radical of a shift in diet can throw you off balance, which is more likely to create overall imbalance than positive change. I do however highly recommend at least for the thirty day period that you change out white flour products for whole grain, refined white sugar for agave or natural organic stevia, and no fried anything. Also refrain from all processed or preservative filled foods, hydrogenated oils, and all soda (diet or regular). These are to be replaced with organic whole fresh local (at least grown within the USA) fruits and vegetables, whole grains, organic extra virgin olive oil (replacing any hydrogenated oils and butter). Use free range organic meat if you do not feel vegetarian is right for you (keeping on the lean and lighter meats and heavy metal safer fish list like wild salmon). Slow change gives the taste buds time to adjust. After a while you may find many cravings subside naturally. Somewhere within the month you may even discover that many lower quality foods begin to taste weird and lose their appeal altogether, as you stick to a healthier routine. Juicing fresh greens, eating raw fresh vegetables and fruits, and increasing fresh high quality lemon water daily will also help this cleanse immensely.

Even with extensive knowledge in nutrition and herbs, I still check with my master herbalist when I am using many herbs simultaneously to know what intervals are best for which herbs. Also note that many medications have contradictions with certain herbs, so again checking with your doctor about mixing or taking any cleansing herbs with any medication is an important consideration. Some tinctures are meant for very short term use, while others are fine to continue with on an ongoing basis. Then (even after attaining professional guidance) you may still feel intuitively guided to stop an herb or product after only a few days. Learn to trust your body's direction alongside sound professional guidance. You are ultimately responsible for what you take into the body so learn what and how much of anything is right for you.

Each color of the 30 day spiral reflects a chakra, and will be explained in detail as we move forth day by day. These colors reflect daily direction on what to eat and wear, plus intuitive instructions on inner work, reflecting each daily body center that we are in. Again I highly recommend journaling your own progress daily. Go buy a beautiful journal, and really take the time to track your diet, sleep, dreams, and personal blocks you may cross as you proceed. Know that any challenges you encounter are merely gifts in disguise from spirit for you to learn and heal from.

Skipping ahead to the charts in the resource guide can also help you to create a grocery list so check recipe ideas ahead of time for each week. I have also included a **thirty day Snapshot Chart** for those of us on the go. Use this to mark your calendar for the month so you can anticipate colors and chakra work ahead of time. Doing this helps to just glance at a single concentrated focus point and be able to move into the day quickly. I have also included several money saving short cuts so you can reuse one meal into the next day, and build daily smoothies from a few base ingredients. I share this to help keep the process efficient and practical in cost. If you can afford it, obviously juicing fresh greens daily would be ideal. For a working, teaching, writing, full time Mom like me, this is not always so practical.

If you are not sure when you want to begin, just look at your calendar to see what day feels right. I would recommend you pick a starting date that is without social commitment. Since my week can be extremely busy, I chose to begin on Sunday so I could ease into this slowly with a lighter schedule. Sunday for me has a little extra personal time to be able to get quiet and focused. Using this pause can help prep for the following week by getting foods, color items, and carving out some personal time to be alone. Another suggestion is to begin with a new moon or going full moon to full moon which will help you align with natural planetary cycles as well.

Another advantage to skipping ahead to the Resource Guide at the end of the book is that each chakra can show you what food items, essences, and therapies can be anticipated in advance. Marking your calendar can help you prepare appointments or personal time needed a few days ahead. I found myself at the health food store saying "okay I need a rooting red food, a sacral strengthening orange item, and some power yellow fun treats." Then I intuitively followed the lead of what would be right for my body. Once you feel you have the foods, essences, journal, and chart ready, just dive in at any point and follow along. You may be guided to add other items or daily "to do's" later, that might feel right for your own progress as you continue. Or you may decide to wait until you can order a few special items online first, before you start your own labyrinth adventure.

Another fun optional item to add is the **Spiral Gemstone kit**. This is a set of ten colored gemstones that work with your chakras and can be used to increase daily awareness and support in each of your centers. These are listed under **therapy stone** in each chakra day in the Resource Guide. These are only examples of good chakra support stones, since there are countless other additional stones for each chakra to help open and shift each center. So if you have other gemstones in mind just add them in. Take the time to prepare at least a day or so in advance to get an overview for each week. Scheduling yourself personal time for this helps keep things organized alongside work, kids, and personal needs, so you know you will remain on track as you get busy.

If you are currently dealing with any drug or

alcohol addiction, please schedule help and extra support alongside this journey. Competent assistance can be very useful when life is overwhelming. This month is meant to be a gentle healing experience for us to be able to joyfully balance and expand in. Increasing our personal wellbeing can be a loving, natural process or an ongoing drama depending on our awareness and intention. If things feel too intense at any point, seek the right support for you can make all the difference. Walking this journey with a trustworthy friend can help support the low points, while celebrating high peaks as well. Going into the core within this process can confront issues we all carry within, that need to be honored, heard, and then lovingly released.

Should you feel resistance here, or are questioning your readiness to begin. You may simply choose to read ahead a few days to study the process and get ideas first. Then when you feel ready and guided to start, just go back to day one to experience this transformation for yourself. Forcing change never works or lasts. If this feels too strange, just walk ahead a few steps so you can observe my process until you are comfortable enough to proceed on your own. Then at some point you will shift and feel your own enthusiasm surface. Your own eagerness means you are ready to start your own work. At this level you can receive the blessings waiting for you as your own inner excavation is complete. Some readers report that they read this entire book in one gulp then went back and felt more confident going step by step through the thirty days. Go at the pace that is right for you.

Also included are daily affirmations to help keep your spirits up, should you feel distracted by your own schedule. I have added meditation prep questions for each day since most people prefer structure. These are all optional journal prompts and therapy ideas, so just take from them what feels right. Staying within the daily focus will clear the chakras energy, and help each center at the level that is right for you in each moment.

Should you choose to buy a recommended item just make sure it feels appropriate for your needs. When you go to any store, should a purchase feels "off or weird" then simply choose something similar that resonates better. Once in your own natural flow (within the labyrinth) you will come across the right people, books, and accents you need along the way. Following this 'now moment' is always hilarious and wild to experience. I never tire of the awe it inspires when one can hold a thought, then literally find its form within a day or two. Trust your ability to manifest exactly what you will need to create your own highest healing experience. Now if you feel prepared and enthusiastic to begin, then take a deep breath and set your whole self into motion. Believe that you can change your life for the better. Know that right this very moment, the entire universe is conspiring to help you heal, love and balance yourself so that you may connect with your divine self and align to your soul path ready to be experienced in the now.

Day One

Day one: inner heart (4th chakra) – pink – center point to begin body spiral - **consciously connecting to your inner heart**.

Journal 6:20 am: Wild dream last night that I was talking to an international airline pilot and introducing him to my Dad? The pilot was tall with dark hair and had a thick athletic build. Although this made no rational sense, (other than boarding for a far journey), I will just stay open to finding guidance here. So without judgment I will just track this dream and move on. Went to my prayer alter this morning to call in the highest healing guidance to hold positive supportive light for me through this month long cleanse.

I personally hold intention to avoid alcohol, coffee, and sugar, while maintaining an organic diet of as much raw fruit and veggies as possible. If you eat meat or have all of these in your diet, please remember that there is no judgment here. I am not here to win anyone over to my own beliefs. Instead I offer and share my own experience to hopefully inspire and support you into better health. Know that even one simple change that is maintained after completing this cleanse, will leave you better off than where you started. Release yourself from constant comparison to anyone around you during this time. Finding what you need and want to achieve will keep your spirits up. Open to align to your own highest quality diet and lifestyle that is right for your current needs. You get to decide what this month means for you, based on your own personal requirements and beliefs.

This morning I was guided to bring a rough tangerine quartz on my walk along the intercoastal where I live in Belleair, Florida. Here many thoughts began to immerge, including the idea of these spirals that kept visually repeating for me to create this project. After my walk I stopped to rest at a nearby jungle trail. I admired the huge overgrown wild oaks completely canopying a beautiful natural Florida wildscaped trail. I glanced around feeling held by this jungle, admiring many species of palms, elephant ears, and wild ginger. I sat with my back to several twenty plus foot bamboo trees, drinking in this tropical forest space. I closed my eyes to hear the bamboo whistle and crack overhead in the wind. Glancing around I noticed a large spider who was sitting in front of me on an enormous elephant ear leaf. "Hello" I smiled, knowing that this was the totem symbol of writers. The spider sat calmly, gazing in a focused manner towards me. I knew that this was confirmation about this creative project sitting before me. "I just finished editing my last book yesterday" I mumbled to myself. "I don't know if I want to start another writing project the very next day." Yet as I walked on, this idea began to pulse and feel more exciting.

(see resource guide)**blushing goddess shake**:
Organic Banana, organic raspberries (or any red fruit)
raw coconut flakes, coconut oil, organic coconut juice
organic hemp seeds or powder
unsweetened pomegranate juice (any red juice)
organic flax seeds (raw sprouted)
fresh pineapple and shredded ginger
liquid b-12 complex +few drops colloidal silver

You can use any vibrational essence that matches your emotional needs. Herbal remedies have can be found at most health food stores, so you can find what remedy tincture is right for you. Linda Nash Stevenson who is a licensed Acupuncture physician and master herbalist who has created a Living the Spiral chakra herbal tincture set to support the chakras energetically on this cleanse (see back for info). Using these can be a powerful assistance energetically to break through stubborn lower emotional patterns.

Once this shake is blended, it creates a light pink shade that reflects this inner heart center. This nourishing shake contains the right nutritional combination to sustain you with high energy for most of the day.

Your chosen shade of pink today represents the gentle reflection of unconditional universal divine love. Allow yourself to disengage from others to be in your own natural rhythm as much as you can today. For those with children, I know this can mean when everyone is asleep. Intend to make time get a quiet rose petal sea salt bath, or to get out under the stars to connect to your own inner heart light today.

The moment I got home from walking, I grabbed a large poster board and my children's crayola markers, immediately scribbling the spirals I was shown earlier. I drew out this complex map and watched in awe as it unfolded into what is now the first chapter of this book. The simple power of intending to heal and open to your own soul work will create the right shifts for you. If we really intend change, then put our best foot forward, we need to be prepared for some collective momentum right around the bend. The universe might just whoosh you into a full spiral that will align you to your own unique path, once you are ready.

Today's color is a soft or rich tone of pink, which resides at the center of the green heart chakra. You may be guided to wear a specific shade of pink, or buy pink roses for your home. Even bathing in a little pink Himalayan crystal salt (health food store), rose petals, or quality rose essential oil will help align you to this frequency more. I like to play instrumental healing or other non-lyrical music while bathing with large rose quartz crystals. Just sit in this pink tone so you can saturate yourself in unconditional love. You can also bless the bathwater through prayer, and call in whatever divine assistance of the highest healing light that feels right for you. Then breathe in from the core of this heart center vibration in your own opening ceremony ritual bath.

The goal of today is to connect to your own spiritual center or God source within. Connecting to this light within every breath will help you to be and stay in flow. This is not a forced reaching from within, but instead a tremendous exhale as though you are relaxing into a seaside hammock supporting you gently from all sides. In letting your own mass go, you can be held and nourished from the love that is all around you at every moment. Breathe in and give yourself the gift of this self-love.

Remember an open heart will instantly align you

to divine source. If you have a rose quartz, I would recommend sleeping with it under your pillow or bed. Bathing and sleeping with rose quartz can also calm and soften your heart while comforting any outstanding inner child issues. The purpose and intention of this ceremonial bath is to connect (even if only momentarily) to the power source of infinite love that resides within us all.

The experience of aligning to your own team of universal support through a loving and safe setting can be enough to help you sustain a strong commitment throughout this thirty day journey. You may even want to write out a contract to spirit including your goals and intentions. Your own soul contract can serve to strengthen you in weak moments throughout the month. I will do my best to guide you along; however it is your own application and follow-through of these suggestions that will ultimately decide your own progress.

Once committed here on both the fun exciting days, and the contrasting not so fun times of change, we must each enter our own core alone. Although seemingly alone, know that you always have infinite support of your guides, angels, animal totems and your own ancestors along the way. They will leave ongoing inspiration to nudge you along, if you are willing to stay open to this support. Especially in times when we forget, then remember, our own divinity again and again through our own blossoming.

A few stones I use and recommend for the heart center are rose quartz, rhodocrosite, green fluorite, and pink tourmaline. Using rose water to spray into your aura, or drinking a floral or rose tea would also soften your field today. If you can find local organic edible flower petals, then eating this essence would be beneficial as well. Wearing pink (even if only a scarf or underwear) will also soften and nourish this center today. For men (don't feel uncomfortable here) you may have a touch of pink somewhere in your house. Even simply adding a pink tone sunset picture to your computer screen at work for the day is fine. Small comfortable accents of any color needed throughout the month will still bring their frequency in for you.

Both masculine and feminine energy exist in the heart chakra, which need to be in balance for the greatest harmony. Many women and men can greatly benefit from balancing the other gender aspect within their own system. We all have the intuitive feminine and the active masculine within us no matter what our sex or sexuality is.

For example, have you ever noticed how deep the voices are for most news anchor women? This deeper voice is a good example of women doing their best to hold their own (accessing this male yang energy), in a predominately male profession. You can hear them drawing out more of the masculine to compete in this field, by accessing this deeper voice (or masculine quality). Understanding this illustration of women very active in their masculine is actually vital and healthy unless they do not counterbalance this for overall harmony. An extreme masculine or feminine trait is not wrong by any means, just optimum when balanced and tempered for greater wholeness.

For men who counsel others and may be accessing their own feminine receptive side constantly, they may benefit from a masculine balancing as well. The point and goal here is to access and balance both of these gender frequencies within your whole self for your own balance. Within our system are the feminine (left side of the body) and masculine (right side) to keep an eye on during this month. Be sure to journal which side of the body any challenges or issues arise for you. From this observance you can find clues to help keep these two sub genders harmonious. Should you find pains or upsets all surfacing out of the left side of your body simply journal the specifics and keep observing. At times these pains may be pointing to messages regarding your ability to receive what is needed in life (or needed feminine balancing work). Obviously there are many variables involved here but the point is to observe what and where issues come up for you physically, emotionally, and spiritually. It is also important to note this so you can begin to follow your own patterns, in order to redirect any blocks out of your own system. Once you understand your own patterns, you then have more insight to answer the questions your body may be asking of you.

Pink represents the divine love of the universe. It is the color of unconditional acceptance, regardless of what you think you deserve or want. We are all divine children, who have everything as soon as we realize it. Whenever I sit outdoors and connect to nature I sense a drinking in of this infinite essence from every direction. There is perfect infinite essence in any cared for natural setting that can be easily passed over, even forgotten in a world addicted to ongoing stimulation from devitalized food and over stimulating entertainment. Nature contains this essence of unconditional love. Connect today outdoors even if it is just walking on a patch of grass for five minutes to remember this fundamental truth.

Consciously breathing in this pink light automatically activates this core in the center of our heart chakra. Today you will trail northward into the first ten day phase to cleanse and clear out your physical body and home.

Day one affirmations:
Today I open and love myself into greater wellness
I deserve vibrant health, joy and peace
I commit to success on this 30 day journey
I allow infinite blessings of divine love
I invite angels of divine love to heal my body and life

Day One meditation questions and prep:

1. What do I intend to personally achieve through this cleanse? Emotionally? Physically? Spiritually? Personally? (setting defined goals in each area can help, or simply journaling thoughts and physical changes each day as you go along)

2. What can I do to open and connect to my highest universal source today? (meditation, breath work, time in nature, ceremonial rose quartz bath)

3. Where if anywhere do I need to go? (local park, appointments to see what level of diet, herbs, cleansing products, exercise is right for you)

4. What pink items do I have or feel compelled to get to assist this opening? (rose quartz, small pink

accent, clothing, make it fun)

5. What do I feel compelled to eat to assist this opening? (Blushing Goddess smoothie, or pink grapefruit, watermelon, or even a pink salad dressing (see spinning lotus dressing in resource guide), purchasing a high quality cleansing program or fiber to help reduce toxins in the system, increasing fresh spring or distilled water, juicing, increasing vegetables and fresh fruits while releasing all stimulants and processed foods)

* See resource guide – chakra list – and snapshot chart at end of book for recipes and daily suggestions.

Day two

Day two: crown center – (7th chakra) – violet – inbound body spiral - **Aligning our intentions for highest healing spiritual support for our physical goals**.

Today we venture above the head into the violet crown chakra. Here we get to align with higher spiritual forces to improve our communication with the divine. No matter how well we are doing here, this is a day to clear out any limiting beliefs about what is possible in universal support and our connection there.

The second day is the largest outer spiral of this physical loop which should still be a comfortable level of introspection. Ask your angels and guides of the highest healing light to help you along the way to hear, see and know what you need to do today.

am journal: What a strange dream! Honestly I initially thought to myself there is no way I can journal this here. After taking time to meditate I received insights that put this dream into higher perspective (hence the crown chakra day of seeking higher perspective guidance for all things which may not make logical sense).

Okay so here goes. In the dream I went out into my back yard and was walking around. Only to discover that our neighbors that live behind us had removed our entire back fencing. This included all of our wonderful palm trees and shrubbery surrounding both sides of the fence completely exposing our property. The entire back portion of our yard was left bare and vulnerable to the active street that ran behind us. At first I thought "maybe they will put up a better fence?" Still I wanted to let them know that cutting our trees and landscaping down was totally uncalled for without our permission.

Next a police officer walked out of nowhere

looking at footprints on the ground. "Is there a problem?" I asked. "Yes, there is someone snooping around in this area... we are working on it," he replied sternly. Now I was anxiety ridden and wanted my fence back up ASAP. Then I shifted into another sequence where I was driving right over our own grass into our back yard (instead of using the street) only to find a new industrial chain link fence replaced our old missing one. The gate in the center was left wide open. I then turned to my right and saw a middle aged man attempting to kick in the back door of our house. I yelled for my husband to help, when the man saw us he began to sprint towards us. I shot straight up wide awake in bed in a cold sweat.

Just for the record, I have always been an extremely vivid and active dreamer since I was a child. Those who know me personally are probably having a good laugh about now (nodding in agreement). Regardless, I was not happy about this rattling. Before even going to the bathroom, I went to the window and checked on our back fence which of course, was still there. Next I prayed for protection and recorded this in my journal while telling myself "I'll just skip this entry for the book." Yet something inside encouraged me to just make notes and step back for a moment. Sometimes dreams are trying to relay important information to assist us. Often they are not literal but symbolic. Other times they are just a much needed mental release of stress.

After completing my daily schedule, I was thrilled to finally get outside. Once under my majestic oak trees outside, I could get still enough for a chance to inquire to my guides about the meaning of this dream. At first I got the image and message of our fence representing old boundaries that were going to be upgraded and expanded. My anxiety was showing the awareness of this process beginning. I knew that this project being a core cleansing, meant that old comfortable patterns (fences) were going to be uprooted and removed, leaving me feeling vulnerable temporarily. Obviously this was being expressed in the dream through "losing my fence." The fence represented my comfort zone or sense of security, as well as my sensitivity to expanding this set zone. When I dropped my defenses in came the ego police, checking on "someone snooping around." Our ego is not usually willing to expand or change, and can attempt to stop the higher self from opening more. I then affirmed that our home and personal space were always safe. When the ego is threatened, it can throw every fear tactic our way to keep control.

Upgrading boundaries are an ongoing task for

every light worker on the planet. Having constantly evolving energetic tools to stay clear are vital for us all. We need to know where to expend our energy, as well as the wisdom for when to conserve our strength. I lightened from this input, remembering there was nothing to fear. While sitting in my yard checking out our fence, I confirmed that it was time to upgrade my life and boundaries. I prayed for a space clearing to release all fear surrounding this issue, then thanked this dream for its message.

I then held onto my amethyst and fluorite crystal while going through my morning meditation. I asked for guidance on this violet day, and was guided to put everything aside to go play. Our guides and angels all want us all to lighten up and laugh more. Play is needed every day and helps to increase our connection to the divine in the long run. I went inside excited to shift this energy into a higher, more fun gear.

I decided to shake off this dream by blasting Elvis music and having a sock sliding party with my kids before starting our home school work. After a few laps around our living room we all felt energized. Together we made a royal smoothie that was the same as yesterday (just with blueberries added) to get the violet shade. I also added some releasing despair vibrational elixir to help flush out any upset from the dream.

Rescue remedy from Bach remedies also works well for emotional upset of any kind. After dressing in a purple vest and keeping these same meditation stones in my pocket, I also decided to wear my amethyst mala beads to strengthen my crown chakra connection throughout the day.

Day two affirmations:
I easily connect to my guides, angels and guardians
It is safe to align to the highest healing light support
I easily align to the divine truth of my soul
Any crown influence not of the highest healing light is immediately cleared and released by my soul

Day Two meditation prep:

1. How well do I connect with my guides and divine healing energy? (make time alone today staying open, journaling to find patterns of insight)

2. What can I do to strengthen my relationship with my guides and angels? (ask questions before sleep, meditation, paying attention to books and information you come across that 'just happens' to be parallel to what you are inquiring about)

3. What can I do to open my crown chakra to

the right amount for my physical development right now? (too wide of a crown chakra is not better and can create imbalance. So gently open to your own appropriate level. Hair washing and brushing stimulates this top of the head area, also yoga poses lotus (or half lotus) while focusing and breathing into this crown area through the pineal point at the top of head, headstands, aligning to stars or lunar energy can open this area to help balance our connection.

4. What can I do today to assist and celebrate this area? What violet, white items or gem stones can I wear or bring with me to cleanse and activate this center? (spirit quartz, amethyst, any jewelry, clothing or accents in this color range)

5. What do I feel compelled to eat or do today? (I prefer solitude as much as possible in the higher centers personally). Obviously a busy job and social gathering is not the place to explore here. Just wait until you get time alone to focus. Eating red grapes, eggplant, red onions, figs, plums, purple basil, cabbage and dark rich radicchio shades of fresh spring mix are all great choices. Juicing purple cabbage with apple, celery, and ginger is a fantastic alkaline tonic that will help you feel divine.

Chapter Two
Further into the loop

Day Three

Day Three: third eye – (6th chakra) – cobalt blue – body spiral - **Stimulating your third eye (brow) chakra increasing personal clarity to support your goals**.

Venturing into the second loop of the first spiral we now engage our third eye. Felt inspired this morning to wear a cobalt blue turtle neck, indigo vest, and tanzanite ring. Last night strange dreams surfaced again in many odd fragments, which I see as a good sign of deep release. To me this was indeed confirmation that my mind is following my intention to heal and clear out the old by dumping out old thought fragments that no longer serve any purpose.

The theme of today seems to be to "clear the head." Of all things I was actually guided to update my year end records (being January for me right now). It feels relevant to clear out old monthly statements etc. from last year for my own personal accounting records. I was guided to release old bank statements, papers, and organize my office to increase clarity in my thinking space. Although you might not be led to do this exact activity, cleaning your working space area can work wonders to clear the head. While organizing to update your records, this energetic shift can bring forth an increased peace of mind and clarity to your personal status. It can also free up your focus and recycle old scattered mental fuel for better use on new creative projects.

At first I resisted pulling out my office files judging that this was "not spiritual enough" for this third eye day theme. Then as I stepped back to observe inner guidance, I realized the physical portion of this spiral is the here and now earth plane. Our sixth chakra mind includes everything we have manifested in our lives physically (or materially) up to this point. Although cleansing is not glamorous, sometimes the mundane tedious overhauls that can take a few hours are well worth it later for ongoing flow.

From the fragments that came forth through my dreams last night, the portion that feels relevant to share (which also prompted my record checking) began at a scene where I was out of town. Suddenly I realized my purse was gone. I returned to the upscale restaurant I was at earlier that evening, but no one there remembered seeing my purse. Then a woman sitting alone (a few tables behind the table I was standing at) pointed to the right. She was hiding her pointing finger with her other hand, which tipped me off to who had my purse in the room. I followed this woman's lead and confidently walked over to a young awkward teen with dark hair, asleep with his head down on the table. Also on the table was a large white bag that I carefully peeked in. I then realized that not just my purse was in this sack, but many others as well. I gingerly pulled my wallet out, trying to stay calm when he woke up startled. Then I let him have it, yelling and scolding him for obviously stealing from many people at once. This morning I forgave the dream but am still going to stay alert (and check all my records).

On my walk today, I saw a huge pod of dolphins which I haven't seen in a while. They swam in circles and played for a long time in front of me which was a blessing to relax to. Especially after so much mental focus was spent earlier, honestly I needed the break. For my diet today I had my usual hemp shake back from chapter one, with added blueberries to create the fun blue shade. Blackberries, pomegranate, and purple cabbage are also indigo foods to open and nourish this center. There is also purple basil or any food or tea leaf that falls into this shade category.

Use and follow what you are drawn to. For some this may be a day of resting your mind (if your job is mentally demanding). For others this is a day of clearing to free up your own mental ram. You will have the energy for what is right for you to engage in, so trust your path.

Day three affirmations:
I release all limited beliefs and thinking today
My mind is open to experience more intuitive sight
I see truth in my life and experiences today
I now release anything keeping me out of clear sight
I understand my divine guidance and know what changes are right for me

Day three meditation questions and prep:

1. What can I do today to clear my third eye center and open my intuitive sight more now? (rub castor oil in circles on the forehead area between your eyes, holistic eye wash, head massage, washing hair, ear candling)

2. What do I need to let go of to allow clearer thinking and easier mental focus? (updating office records, home maintenance clutter, find where you are drawn to first and start there)

3. What cobalt or indigo blue items can I eat, wear, or use today to assist this center to create

balance today? (blueberries, most bluish tones from yesterday, blue malva tea, stones: lapis lazuli, sodalite, fun indigo blue tones in clothing, and any accents you come across that feel right for you)

4. What can I do to support this center more? (Om chant, minimizing or eliminating TV, being in nature more, yoga poses include seated forward bends, head to knee forward bends, all positive visualizations with healing breath, toning and any sound healing work)

5. What do I need to know or see today on my path? (asking for your next step to clear out the old, scheduling counsel or support you may need, quiet time to align to your own inner guidance)

Day Four

Day four: throat center – (5th chakra) – sky blue –body spiral – **Throat chakra expressing physical changes and goals to others who will support you**.

I tend to give the throat chakra area special attention because of having personal fifth chakra body and spiritual challenges in the past. Going through challenge here has taught me a great deal, after many years of suffering from thyroid dysfunction. For me this was the physical price of not speaking or living my truth in life. Continually stifling my spirit and abilities created a physical debt from suppressing my own creative expressions for too long. I know I am an "out there visionary thinker" but would just keep it all inside because of my sensitivity to others response to my gifts. I used to catch myself editing constantly what I really saw and felt, trying to keep others comfortable around me. Over time this behavior was suppressive and extremely detrimental to several chakras of my body. Eventually this manifested quite a system imbalance, until I was willing to change my own patterns.

My healing took bold strides of speaking up without editing my true personal beliefs. The next step was then sharing without apology about what I really wanted out of life. When I finally put my own health and spiritual path first (and got out of obligated groups and social situations), my entire endocrine system balanced out on its own in record time. I now understand the price of "playing nice" is too high for any of us. When I began to tell everyone what I really thought, wore my funky sarongs and danced under the moonlight, I felt great. My own natural rhythm returned to balance. I walked away from many people, places, and habits that were not building my energy but in fact expending my physical self and life force, at a terrible price.

These bold strides reactivated and regenerated me enough to not only get off medication, but to also maintain this balance now almost a decade later. This period blessed me with a hypersensitive crash course to better understand and monitor my own unique bio rhythm. Learning how to work with and balance your chakras daily is a preventive health measure to keep your whole self-balanced.

When the throat chakra is balanced and activated we can sing, write or create anything appropriate for our path. Once we get our inner spicket going, anything is possible. Extremely therapeutic ways to balance and open this area are singing, toning, sound healing, writing, painting and or any craft that is of free expression. Wearing a rich sky or topaz blue in any form also helps to support this throat area. While I was in my own healing process within this chakra, I bought a lot of clothing in this sky blue range. This helped to 'color support' my thyroid, even wearing bright blue flip flops daily.

Kyanite is a sky blue stone that I am particularly fond of (partially because it does not need to be cleared), but also in that it supports this chakra to gently heal inner conflict. It stabilizes our ability to express from the throat center, to rebuild power you may have been giving away or denying in life. You can also wash your hair with organic grape shampoo. Organic grape can sooth and nourish the scalp while the natural aromatherapy of this natural scent calms the mind. Head massage and or gently massaging the ears also relaxes this area with several calming acupressure points. Sound healing is also an amazing modality when applied to any chakra, but obviously moves the throat energy well since our voice resides here. Blue lace agate is another excellent throat gemstone that helps gently activate higher awareness of our daily speech patterns. I find it supplements this area in a supportive soft tone to help strengthen our voice.

pm journal: Today was an unusual pace. Morning mediation guided me to listen and talk as little as possible throughout the day. "Be silent" was my inner direction. For some this might seem constrictive, or even repressive. As I followed this inner lead and observed my interactions with others, I noted internally where I wanted to jump in and speak for others. Being a triple conduit myself I know I can communicate for and with everyone else in a way that can be depleting for me, if I am not aware of where my energy is going.

Not that we shouldn't help others, on the contrary. The point here and key to balancing any center is to use our power and energy wisely. Otherwise we can pull ourselves off our own track by expending too much energy on others around us, which seemed to be the lesson of the day for me to observe in my own work.

Watch your own surroundings today. Observe then journal your own rhythm, while letting things be. Intend to become even more discerning in the jumping in (or rescuer) side that many of us tend to share. Unless of course you are guided to do so by spirit. The stimulation we are all subjected to in public and through mass mind is enough to keep anyone in constant fifth chakra reaction. Or worse shut down all together in order to maintain indifference (in attempt to protect ourselves). Stability is the key to harmony in every chakra. As we increase our awareness about where our energy is continually going, we will find and maintain balance.

Sitting by the intercoastal today with several blue lace agate stones, helped to gently open and nourish my throat center. I watched several pelicans swoop and dive while fishing in the ocean before me. Silence was what I personally needed today to regenerate and rest my throat. For you, an outer expression, or long overdue communication with another may be more important than silence. Remember that our words hold power beyond our comprehension. Even though some of us are opening and respecting this power, there is always a higher level of thought and conscious expression to be realized.

Drank grape Kombucha today, which is a cold Chinese cultured live enzyme tea made by Synergy. Other bright blue foods and herbs for the day are wild indigo, lavender, blueberry tea, as well as ginger that all stimulate the throat nicely. Obviously this does not need to be every meal; even one small item in the day would be great. Just stay open to finding fun alternatives and compliments to your normal routine, while making this a fun game. Stay open to books you just happen to pass and notice. As well as new ideas and alternatives that will step forth for you each day as they are needed. When we allow greater flow in every chakra we get better efficiency out of our whole system. So enjoy your day and make it count.

Day four affirmations:

I speak my truth with ease and faith

I communicate better everyday

I speak up and live my true nature

I am willing to change what is not working in my life

Today I creatively express joyful love

Day four meditation prep:

1. What can I do today to balance and open this center? (voicing or journaling any repressed information that guidance leads you to, or creating new expressions)

2. Who do I need to speak to in order to clear my throat? (anything you are biting your tongue about? holding in creatively? Repeated mind doodling that you need to express through journaling, or sketching)

3. What creation does my throat center want to express? (writing, painting, singing, speaking, all come from this area, yoga poses include neck rolls, camel pose, plow pose)

4. What sky blue items feel right to wear, use or create? (this color range in one or many items such as kyanite, blue topaz, larimar, blue lace agate)

5. What diet will support and heal this area today? (continue with blue accents, purple tone spring

mix, blue malva, I find blueberry smoothies are easiest to create this color)

Day Five

Day five: heart center – (4th chakra) – emerald green – center of body spiral - **Sharing generously while equally receiving the support you need from the universe**.

Ahhhh.... love, what life is all about when we can give and take in a balanced whole fashion. On the other hand, when we take on others pain, grief, or get stuck in pity party negativity, the heart center can get cloudy and stagnate in a heartbeat. It can even shut down or cramp all at once creating a stroke if we are not careful. Clearing the heart today is divinely in the center of this first spiral because although every organ is vital, the heart is the core of our physical function. Our heart center translates upper and lower body information so it is imperative to have it clear and circulating well.

"Taking heart" is a literal term we commonly use to evaluate what is important in life, reminding us to count our blessings. Today is a day to rejoice for the infinite blessings that we all have, and at times can take for granted. Give thanks today for your eyes, hands, ability to walk, talk and share. We assume oxygen is just going to be there for our next breath. We assume the water supply, and other resources are all infinite. Our blessings are truly immeasurable. When we really put an effort forth to acknowledge even just a few of these infinite blessings surrounding us, we often realize we have a lot more going for us than we give due credit.

The fourth chakra center is a beautiful emerald green which reminds me of the surreal tropical portion of Kauai up around Hanalei in Hawaii. Breathing in this vibrant green is the name of the game today. Green foods are easy to find, and being high on the alkaline scale they are very balancing to the entire body. If it is possible, go get a wheatgrass shot, fresh organic green salad, or fresh sunflower sprouts. If it's alive and green, go for it. Today I will wear an emerald Gaia stone, and take chrysoprase, moss agate, aventurine, and green fluorite out for a spin. I have also found bathing with different stones (ck to make sure they do well in water first) can also infuse and open vortexes in and around the body. Sometimes this is very subtle, other times very powerful.

Another way to open and expand this center

today is to write or call a loved one you have not had time to get in touch with for a while. Expressing sincere love from the heart whether it be to your family, friends, nature, or animals can nourish and expand your own heart, so be generous. Since we are coming to the center of the first spiral today, this may be a strong sensation for some of you. In any vortex near the center many can feel the magnetic pull from the vortex center. If you are really following this course and applying the actions daily, I am confident you will have a positive experience here today. Affirming your own inner heart shift can be very healing as you increase your own level of self-care, resulting in greater self-love.

I dressed in head to toe green today. For breakfast I prepared a blue green algae shake with my normal berry hemp combination. Then after lunch my kids made a fresh organic kale, celery, lemon, and apple combo in the juicer. I call it the "grass hopper" for my son and "tinker bell juice" for my daughter. This is also a great alternative to soda for kids. When you add sparkling water to it they think it tastes like sprite so that works for me! Remember all recipes are in the resource guide in back.

For matters of the heart, I am reading Gary Renard's "Your Immortal Reality." Being a student in the Course in Miracles I work on forgiveness daily. So this being a day of the heart is a good time to take inventory on where we all could forgive more. Recently my husband and I were going through a business challenge. I now realize that my initial dream of the man kicking in the backdoor was a business associate confronting us aggressively which I experienced in dream state, just before it happened literally. The gift of being a Course in Miracles student at this time has been invaluable for me to stay on course with forgiveness through this period. Forgiveness work is priceless when others seem to do things that, well....create immense opportunities for us to forgive them.

Trust that whatever positive, inspiring material you are drawn to is right for you to study today. Or perhaps if you feel a little stagnate, venture out and see what books you happen to come across. A book or two may even fall off the shelf near you, only to discover they are exactly what you need to read at this time. Balance in this center is the difference between constant miscommunication of the body and mind, or a fluent natural understanding of your own rhythm and path.

If your heart is clogged, important information may not be making it up or down your system. You can experience a smooth journey while going through your own natural ebbs and flows, without drowning in everyone else's undertow of neediness. In a world where many are looking to take whatever they can get, having clear heart boundaries are mandatory for us all. Most important today (since this is going into the core of our physical self), is to love, love, love your whole self. Love your body including every cell, curve, wrinkle, AND yes your cellulite. Love your work, your family, your friends, your bills, those who cut you off in traffic, anyone living or participating in fear, and for every breath and blessing in between, both seen and unseen around you. All we can give to anyone is our own conscious love of a healthy body, mind and spirit.

Forgive yourself
and everything behind you
to let this be
a whole new day.

Day five affirmations:
I love and forgive myself and others today
I love myself enough to commit to positive change
I balance my give and take today
I give myself permission to love myself and others fully
I safely connect to others with an open heart

Day five meditation prep:

1. Who do I need to forgive today? (who, or whatever comes to mind is where to begin)

2. What will open and or balance this center today? (deep breathing with arms outstretched wide, meditation, being in nature)

3. Where can I give today to make a difference around me? (calling a loved one, old friend, significant letters, charitable donations, volunteering)

4. What is my passion here? (connect through journaling or meditation to increase passion in your life, daydream)

5. What can I eat, wear, or use in the emerald or bright green tones to assist this opening and healing today? (wheatgrass, organic spring mix salad, green melon, grapes, stones: malachite, aventurine, green fluorite, any green jewelry or clothing accent.)

Chapter Three
Full Moon Ceremony

Day Six

Day six: inner heart center – (4th chakra) – pink – outbound body spiral - **Consciously creating a deeper connection of universal flow in life**.

Today is an exciting day of reawakening, as we begin the uncoiling process of this first spiral. Tonight is the full moon (for me here), but not necessarily for you where you are following along lunar/calendar wise which is fine. Although hopefully you can enjoy the outdoors tonight and there will be starlight visible for your own experience. Today this rose light again springs forth to awaken and ignite us gently from within.

Now beginning the outward phase of the first spiral, this is a time to be gentle and extra nurturing with your body. The rose color also represents the lotus within the inner heart which you may or may not see in your meditations. When I am closed off or upset about something (then visually check my own heart center), there is no sign of this gentle spinning within. Other times when I feel extremely connected or am doing an earth ceremony, I find this not only opens but strings of golden whitish colors lengthen from within it to open along my entire body. What is important here regardless of what you see or feel is to keep your heart open to receive more from the universal flow.

Today may ignite the urge to wear pink, or have this color near you in some way. I find fresh flowers (especially pink orchids or roses) to be perfect for this experience. The power of pink knows no limits. Being such a gentle vibration, some say pink is a weak or vulnerable color. Yet in my opinion, the soft pink of rose quartz for example, is one of the most powerful stones because this often quiet, unpretentious power of love does truly conquer all.

I also find it interesting that pink is the sponsor color of the woman's breast cancer fund. The power of so many women coming together to create a collective vibration from the symbolic healing pink ribbon shows us that love is stronger than any disease within. The darkest corners of our life and self when put next to the soft rose will begin to melt over time. In this vibration everything will eventually soften. Rose quartz is an incredible stone to support your home or office.

Other great pink stones include rhodocrosite, pink tourmaline, or pink topaz. Again if these do not feel necessary to use, then just skip them and move on.

Another wonderful indulgence I mentioned earlier for you today is a beautiful bouquet of pink roses (I picked a rich pink blush shade myself). If there is any day to add roses or fresh flowers, this is it. Doing this will open and soften your field (which we can all benefit from). Everyone hears "lighten up," which by all means is important, especially when it comes to the ability to laugh at ourselves. Yet to "soften up" is to breathe in our soul connection. Then to exhale fully and settle into the source of all creation, knowing and trusting that we are safe and cared for in every breath.

Another addition to a sea salt bath could be a pink Himalayan rock salt, rose petals, or any additional flower or chakra herbal tincture essence that feels right for you to add. In looking for school supplies for my daughter this morning I happened upon a bottle of the Bach remedy Willow that was tucked in the corner of the closet out of sight. Willow helps us vibrationally to move through deep unforgiveness patterns or resentments (which I happened to find on the inner heart day). This Bach remedy on a green or pink day is ideal and may help you cycle through any residue of unforgiveness within this center. Willow is also an excellent remedy for going through any relationship break up, or any other situation of unforgiveness, that may still be animating shadow remains in your heart center.

am journal: Woke up feeling quite fragile this morning. Although my impulse was to jump into chores and my usual "to do's" for the day, a whisper asked for a few more minutes of silence first. So I sat on the floor with a large rose quartz, with gentle healing music flowing in front of me and remained still. I could see that the throat silence of yesterday had restored my fifth chakra for the better. I knew today was going to be a powerful internal shift, although honestly I just felt vulnerable and cautious on the outside.

I saw a strong visual of color going through this spiral aligning with my intention. Know this entire process will shift each of us on a deeper level that has nothing (and yet everything) to do with our body. I then saw a swirling pink pinwheel like image that spun at first tightly angled then opened in to a circular swirling momentum. I knew this was a release of confined control in my own heart affecting my own connection to source. Any tenderness or sense of fragility that may come forth momentarily today in the heart center may be showing a guarded nature or withholding of love in some way. We cannot be expanding and guarded simultaneously (hence my own sharp angles). Encourage your heart to allow this internal light to gently melt where you may be holding back from yourself or others. Then open tenderly to more of the unlimited love that you too may choose to let in after softening any guardedness or blocks that may surface in your own field.

Tonight (on my calendar) is the full moon. I am going to create a fun ceremony to celebrate this exciting night. After a rough interlude with our business, my family is taking an 'at home vacation' weekend. Going to the beach to clunk down in the sand is a wonderful break for me. Give yourself permission to shirk your chores this weekend (or coming weekend) and let yourself have a vacation free from your ordinary routine. Sometimes simply getting out of our element and going anywhere different helps to open our heart as we realize there is life and well deserved relaxation, beyond our circle of routine.

I prepared for the full moon ceremony by intuitively gathering several candles of different shades. I then added a few crystals and a silver coin. I went to our side yard where I meditate, to sit under a grand oak that canopied over me in every direction. I was a little concerned initially because of the overcast weather throughout the afternoon. At first it did not even look like a full moon night because of the layer of clouds blanketing the entire sky. I then asked for guidance about whether to continue setting up, and felt assurance that there would be a window of opportunity.

Feeling enthusiasm wellspring from within I began prepping a large spiral labyrinth with a Moon goddess candle infused with essence of lemongrass, lavender, and ylang ylang at the center. Around it I was guided to the proper placement of the stones and candles with one candle and stone in each of the coils. I began with a prayer of invocation for guidance and high integrity direction throughout the ceremony. I was guided to enter circling to the left slowly, yet deliberately. Through each ring I thanked God, Goddess, Christ, my guides, ancestors, Mother Earth, St Germain, Babaji, Buddha, my Huna family, Archangel Michael, Raphael, and the entire angelic realm. I also included the mineral, elemental, animal, and fairy kingdoms. As well as the nature spirits, light beings and elements in gratitude for their constant support as well.

As I reached the center I felt quite disoriented. So I stopped and held firm intention to heal at a deeper level through this cleanse at every level of my being. I gave thanks for all of the blessings and protection the universe has poured forth throughout my entire life. I asked for assistance on the many creative projects I have been engaged in this past year (including this book). I prayed for the moonlight to infuse them all with strength and wisdom. I asked that these books and projects would empower and heal as many as possible, while also magnetizing those who would benefit from this cleansing process.

I then circled out in the opposite direction, thanking Mother Earth at the end for supporting this healing. Finally I buried a coin at end of the last ring, to honor Mother Earth for holding this symbol. Before blowing out the candles in each ring of the coil, I admired first how beautiful they were glimmering in the dark making this a sacred event indeed. The divinely wild outcome here was that just as I began my walk, the clouds shifted just enough allowing full moonlight to grace me into the spiral. After that (although clouds passed over in patches) the moon kept peeking through continually throughout the process. Then as I prayed to close the ceremony and blew out the candles, I glanced up to the perfect radiant full moon I had initially hoped for.

After finishing I packed up and still wanted to lay out for a moon bath. So I sat out with one candle lit to pray and relax. When I realized the moon was now long gone behind the cloud cover I had started out with before. I waited for about fifteen minutes or so until I realized I was indeed blessed to have the short miracle window for my labyrinth ceremony. I then took a long rose quartz crystal bath adding fresh rose petals, and again became still.

Practicing stillness is an art that most in our society may scoff at, yet for me this is the connection key. Our divine power is always waiting in the stillness. Whenever we are finished racing about, we may drop down exhausted. Only to find that what we had been searching for has been waiting quietly within us all along.

Day six affirmations:
I allow divine flow to lead me today
I integrate divine love into my system with ease
I surrender to divine will in all things today
I breathe in pure divine light in every breath
I relate to everyone from an open radiant heart

Day six meditation prep:

1. How can I consciously align to this divine flow more? (opening awareness to love in everything and everyone around you in every moment)

2. What would help you to experience this divine presence more in your life every day? (new commitment to meditation, breath work, visualization)

3. What is priority here for your inner heart alignment and experience? (time alone is crucial to explore and know your own truth before working with others)

4. What can I accent with today? (pink flowers, goddess shake –see resource guide for recipe, pink clothing, accents, rose quartz)

5. How can I get extra reassurance about this process ? (ask for the universe to show you a sign you are on path and then watch for it closely, journal when you find or dream about it)

Day seven

Day seven: solar plexus center – (3rd chakra) – yellow – outbound body spiral - **Directing your will and focused strength from your power center more efficiently**.

After an interlude to refill from source, the next stop is to pour that self-love right into your solar plexus to balance your sense of self-esteem. This is meant both within us, and out to the world around us. Our third chakra is located just above the navel, and is a brilliant sunny yellow. Here we may find power struggles can occur with others from this chakra, as our egos wrestle about with others in all sorts of ways. Of all of the places to clear negative tethers from, this is a popular center where you can usually find the most cords. There are many wonderful techniques to clear out this (and all of your centers). You can use prayer, intention, sage, gemstones, or call in the angel realm for assistance. You can ask other high integrity angelic beings to help shift lower blocks to release unhealthy cords keeping you tied to people and places that are negatively affecting your own progress in life.

Power projects today may include anything that enhances your self-esteem. Weight resistance training is good so you can experience your own increasing strength physically. I enjoy yoga handstands and do these often. These poses engage my full body weight while feeling my own inner strength grow from supporting my own weight in a literal sense. Yellow is also a day of enhanced memory and logical process which makes it a great color to engage and activate the mind. Detailed information can be assimilated well today when our power center is up and running well.

Yellow stones that can help energetically are citrine, rainbow moonstone, or yellow topaz. All of these stones help to replace negativity with joyful encouragement to boost this center immediately. How can we not smile and lift when bold grinning sunflowers come our way? Yellow is like the no nonsense friend who strides in and gets the show on the road. It is the color of cutting through and getting to the point. If you ever put on a bright yellow shirt you can even feel this charge when you look in the mirror. For many wearing yellow is a challenge because they may not be comfortable in their own power. Or perhaps you do not care to wear strength around others, and prefer to stay muted in the background more. Sometimes this is a very wise choice and use of power.

If you find you have no yellow items in

your closet, or perhaps dislike yellow all together you may want to explore why? Ask yourself to honestly account where your self-esteem is? See if giving your power to everyone else is a common occurrence, (which we all experience from time to time) so please do not judge or criticize yourself here. Just make notes to improve this center no matter where you are. This may be the exact color you need to assist your reprogramming back to self empowerment and greater self reliance.

Bananas, pineapple, ginger, yellow lentils, lemons, grapefruit, and other yellow herbs and foods are great additions to the diet today. Yellow is also a natural anti-depressant. Although watch painting too strong of a shade in your bedroom (like I did once) because it can over engage your mind and keep you up thinking and processing through the night, instead of sleeping. Too bright yellow or gold in the kitchen can also keep you eating, hence every fast food logo. Otherwise it is the cheery optimism the world needs daily so bring in some healthy sunshine today.

am journal: Guided this morning to walk alone along my jungle path with a large piece of yellow gold citrine and moonstone. It was raining today and pretty gloomy out as I began my trail. I tuned into my power center and just stayed open for guidance. Out of nowhere a wellspring of childlike bubbly giddy joy surfaced and buoyed me along.

After yesterday's deepening in connection to the divine, I realized today is a day of exuberance and optimism that can outshine any gloomy environment, or circumstance. I sat in my usual spot to visit with my grandma oak and realized I could hear at least twenty plus varieties of birds around me. I live in a bird sanctuary, so this is really an immense blessing to have a day that was quiet enough to really enjoy it all to myself (thanks to the overcast weather). Often times this park is so busy with dogs and children (while powerboats zip back and forth in the intercoastal) in front of where I sit. So this privilege of a day alone made me feel as though I was deeper in nature than simply within a few trees. I felt like an awestruck child discovering a magical forest path for the first time. In this setting I realized there was nowhere else I would rather be in the entire world on this morning. There was nothing to go get, achieve, or prove anymore. I was perfectly content, and found the jewel of this peace lies in simply aligning to our own inner nature. Doing the best we can on our path in every breath, can create happiness and incredible fulfillment within. Back from the trail I made a my hemp shake with flax, banana, fresh pineapple, coconut juice shreds, blue green algae, cranberry juice.

Day seven affirmations:

I have excellent self esteem

I call back my power from ______ (can be any person, place, or life circumstance)

I choose a healthy level of power in life

I am self reliant, happy, and capable

I create and share with joy in full esteem today

Day seven meditation prep:

1. What do I need to do today to balance or strengthen my self esteem? (time alone to connect to inner power, strength training, bright apparel)

2. Where do I need to take back my power in life? (rethinking boundaries needed with people, or places you go)

3. How can I overcome low esteem issues by committing to a healthy change today? (releasing any habits not expressing self love, prioritizing time for self, taking the lead where you need to)

4. How can I brighten the day of another today and bring more joy into the world today? (sharing sunflowers or brightening another's day with a note, or fresh baked treat, spontaneous surprises for yourself or others)

5. What can I eat, wear, or use to assist this process of empowerment today? (strength training, climbing, wearing bright shades in this yellow range, citrine, yellow topaz, canary yellow diamonds (why not!) okay perhaps even just a picture of yellow diamonds, moonstone, or any additional accent or yellow food)

Chapter Four
The Outbound journey

Day Eight

Day eight: sacral center – (2nd chakra) – orange – outbound body spiral - **Resetting physical boundaries in the sacral chakra to better support your body and personal needs**.

am journal: Woke up furious at myself. What the heck happened last night? While preparing for dinner of yellow steamed lentils and garlic spinach, I gave in to a glass of red wine. This quickly turned into two glasses, and then continued further off track with taking out the kids for ice cream (which I too would indulge in). The real slap in the face was found this morning as I realized that I had left my entire purse open in the car.

Especially while cleansing, you may find an increase of sensitivity to alcohol which really should be avoided or at least minimized this month (and no I didn't drive). I also noticed that my wallet had fallen out with all of my personal information exposed across the floor of the passenger side of the car. "Thank goodness," I thought trying to pull myself together to move through this now intensifying cloud of self repulsion. "Why did I drop the ball here? I'm cleansing and need to be the example here!" I scolded myself sternly.

We then decided to go to the beach together as a family. My kids ran off to fly kites with my husband while I trailed northward for a walk to clear my head. I brought along my large tangerine quartz, carnelian, and citrine to gather strength and gain insight from this "slip." As I walked along the shoreline, I began to go through my chakras to balance for the day. I felt this anxiety and upset surge within me as a raging swell. When I inquired about what was going on, I was shown the answer would be found later in a past life regression session. I knew later that afternoon I would have time to clear at a deeper level. I was told this upset was connected to a past pattern I had yet to clear at a cellular level.

As I proceeded through each center I realized that my heart chakra had not only bled into my third center, but I also saw that my second chakra was quite squished as well. Without this open and spinning, I know there is an unforgiveness at some level going on, obviously towards myself for this offense. This morning was the first day in a while that my heart center was closed and muddy from my own harsh self judgment earlier. Although oddly my heart energy was also out all over the place searching and running amok, instead of tight to the body and dark as I would expect to see it after such an emotional upset. Perhaps this heart center energy out everywhere was this past life pattern surfacing and bleeding out through this center? I was not sure?

I felt very discouraged this morning as I walked along, even scorning that I was unworthy of doing this project at all. I even considered ditching the book entirely since I was not doing it perfectly, when I felt a tremendous wave from within charge forth to reassure me. Guidance revealed that this slip was part of why I am completely capable and humanly qualified of sharing my own imperfect journey. My guides showed me how many other well meaning readers may actually slip here and there too, leaving them feeling inadequate to continue in this very same way. But through my own example of moving forward without giving up, that you now reading this work may be inspired to not give up where you may be less than perfect in your own spiral cleanse as well. We are here to be real in each present moment. The real goal is to keep our integrity high and our love flowing, no matter where we are in our own process.

Although this down morning did initially prompt judgment, I found myself switching gears quickly accepting this support to get right back on track. On my day of personal power (although technically the slip was on the sacral day where addictions tend to surface from) this was interesting insight to observe a disengaging somehow of my own power, followed by sabotage in my own progress. The goal of this month is to come out in greater health and balance than wherever you started. Should you have a day with less than desired results, or go through a period where you fall into automatic with your own diet or life choices, please forgive yourself. You may want to stomp your feet and declare your own upset. Yes, do that. Express yourself truthfully in each moment, but then get right back into the saddle.

In my walking meditation along the coast, I invoked assistance while admiring the ocean while feeling the warm sand squish between my toes. I instantly felt my entire self (even watching a visual in between the cells) which begin to open and stretch in every direction absorbing an abyss of light. When this light became too intense, I snapped back to the present moment to find whatever was such a big deal beforehand was now suddenly ridiculous, (or at least insignificant) after being in this radiance. Once back from this visual my entire field was instantly clear, as I reconnected my footing to move forward.

I continued back southward mesmerized by the gentle swish of the incoming tide, until I came across a large seahorse washed up in front of me. At first I assumed (since it was washed up so far on the beach) that it was dead. Then as I moved closer to pick it up, it opened the eye facing me and curled its tail in to a swirl. "Oh little fella, let me help you," I cooed as I gently scooped him up and set him back into the shallow tide. I have grown up and walked on the beach since I was born and have never seen a seahorse in the ocean before this day. I continued back to my family then plunked into the sand to watch my kids joyfully finish their sand castles. We all enjoyed the blessing of being together on this quiet weekend to play and soak in the intelligence of the brilliant Floridian sun. Once home I whipped up a:

ray of sunshine smoothie

fresh organic pineapple, papaya, coconut, goji berry, hemp seed, fresh garden mint, ginger, flax seed, banana, and unsweetened cranberry juice.

Since the second chakra holds the element of water I have also purchased a few bottles of oxygenated water for the day (local health food store). As well as being in and around the ocean (or any body of water if possible) also nourishes this water element. As the day progressed I felt inclined to deep clean my car, and create an organic baby basket for my new born nephew. These projects moved artistic energy in a direction of positive creation (even simple cleaning is reorganizing energy to free up creative space).

Today is day one of phase two on my herbal cleanse. I am now releasing one meal a day and increasing fiber and herbs to cleanse at a deeper level. It is important to remind ourselves that ongoing clutter in our life can show up as digestive blockages and or constipation. As we hold on to unnecessary items instead of flowing and releasing the old, we can clog internally. Equally important is maintaining organization of our things in order to keep our clarity, and our energy steady.

Today is an excellent day to create a goodwill donation bag, or library donation of old books and so on. Ask spirit to guide you to what or where you can de-clutter in your own living or work space. You may be surprised where you are led. When I asked this question I was shown our silverware that I had inherited a few years back. Although beautiful, I never cared for using it (or any other antique quite honestly). I saw an image of sharing the grief and emotions of past family members who ate with them. I knew these silverware pieces contained a denser energy infused into them over time. Don't get me wrong here, I love my relatives. I simply did not wish to eat off their silverware (or share energetically from this old template) any longer. Especially since eating issues have been a challenge for me in the past, this made it a particularly sensitive item to feel confident about. So I packed it all up, and bought a new package of contemporary silverware later in the afternoon. The new modern design was a pleasant clean slate of energy that I now feel wonderful using.

This may sound silly to some, even absurd or disrespectful to others. Yet to those sensitive enough to the items in your environment, you too may be aware of imprints you can feel when borrowing items from others. I have slept on guest beds only to have horrible nightmares from the energetic residue of those who had slept there before me. I can intuit that those sitting or lying there before me were either physically ill, grief stricken, and so on. I now steer clear of used clothing, antiques, or any used items unless I am certain that it is of equal or higher vibration. Please understand that this is not snobbery, but simply keeping a high standard of energy. When you respect a high standard, it keeps an overall harmony to your body and personal space that we all deserve to be living in.

PM past life regression: Revisited a past life in rural England. My initial eye view began high on a hilltop overlooking a huge countryside farm. I stood looking out over fields that went on for miles noticing the sea far off in the distance, from the highest hill point. I had on very old worn out brown boots and a homely bluish grey dress. As I walked into my home at the time, we had a unique stone set floor that was dirty. There was an oversized kettle in the corner, and a huge pile of fire wood that was replenished often and used daily. In this simple home I realized my younger sister in this past life was the friend in this life (whom I have had ongoing boundary challenges with) but never quite got a grasp on the dynamic of our friendship (in this life).

In this past life, I knew that out of the two of us, she was "chosen" (therefore more loved and worthy) to school, while I simply worked the farm. I never learned to read while she was schooled (by a neighbor who came to our home) so she could develop skills for a basic education. After which she decided to not continue but instead married and had children of her own. I resented the fact that she was the favored child given this educational opportunity, while I was stuck being the work horse for the farm. Since we were the only two children, our parents needed at least one of us full time running the immense daily workload. So being the physically stronger of the two of us, I became the farmhand.

I spent most of my time alone, and separated myself from others in town out of a constant sense of inferiority. I later died of a stroke. After viewing this menial life, I realized that I felt oddly obligated to this friend in this life out of that continued subconscious sense of inferiority that her schedule, personal needs, and time took priority to my own. Our dynamic (in this life) never made sense to me, and I often commented that if anyone else acted like this friend disregarding my time and schedule, I would read them the riot act then walk away without looking back. Yet this strange unspeakable undercurrent between us (in both this past and current life) kept us entangled in an unspoken 'no boundaries' game in a way that kept me out of my own normal comfort zone and feeling continually disempowered around her.

I took steps to forgive and release this

past life, while forgiving the illusion that I was inferior to her in this life. Being a self worth wound, I could now connect the dots to another possibility why my "wine slip" may have happened on this third chakra day to cope with this sense of inferiority. After a process of release, I reaffirmed a higher cellular intelligence here and let this past life go for good. Acknowledging this line of time where it was harming me today through lowered esteem was important to do, so it could then be redirected out of my cellular patterns in this life. Releasing this entanglement would help to repair my esteem in this life now by releasing this repeating 'loop' with my friend which was disempowering me and repeating a pattern of self sabotage in the now.

I share this personal session with you here as an example of the power and healing potential that is available to us in competent past life regression therapy. Sometimes seemingly impossible dynamics with people or circumstances often stem from past life triggers that keep semi or even subconsciously looping in our cellular memory. If not untangled this "loop" continues until we can disrupt these patterns and redirect ourselves into greater wellness and balance. Many brilliant healers and medical intuitive speakers have written extensively about this, and have professionally documented thousands of cases of personal improvement if health and personal wellbeing improvement from past life therapy success. In personally assisting hundreds of people to help clear their own past life records, I have seen incredible physical and emotional healings occur as a result of this work. Past life therapy is finally getting the respect it deserves and can be life altering to say the least, should you feel it is right for you to engage in with qualified assistance.

Day eight affirmations

I have excellent boundaries with everyone

I easily honor my limits with everyone

I respect my space and needs everywhere

I easily assimilate the changes I need to make

I now strengthen my ability to process energy

Day eight meditation and prep:

1. What or who do I need to upgrade my boundaries with? (friends, family, co-workers, ask for guidance to do so with love)
2. How can I improve my boundaries everywhere? (committing to taking responsibility for your energy and where it is going at all times)

3. What would strengthen my digestive system? (sit-ups, digestive enzymes, probiotics, good posture all help this area to properly function)

4. How can I improve my boundaries out in public? (calling in protection, staying vigilant of your feelings in places, around people then honoring direction on how to deal with them)

5. What do I need to let go of to heal this center? (releasing the need to control people, circumstances, helps us to let spirit 'digest life' with and for us more)

Day nine

Day nine: base center – (1st chakra) – red – outbound body spiral - **Increasing physical stability in your base chakra to maintain balance within the changes you are creating**.

am journal: Woke up with a raw sore throat. Sometimes after going through any past life regression or intense interactive shamanic journeying, the integration time following sends cellular waves that can take a period of adjustment for us to process. We can redirect our cells and DNA as messages travel through many layers of fields in and around our whole being.

There are many wonderful red items that can get the base chakra moving and decongesting today. Try a wonderful warming tea that supports the entire system today organic spices or red hibiscus with a little added agave. Or you can use the Chanakara's 1st chakra tea. You can also add the first chakra essence to support any emotional issue you are intending to clear in the base center. I added a power shot of raw camu camu to help support my own endocrine function, after a lot of emotional output was extended through this work. Spicy red cayenne pepper beckons a wakeup call, especially when you purchase a high dose heat at your local health food store. Cayenne is wonderfully warming and soothing to the throat, and can loosen congestion in the whole system.

Wow talk about life giving ample opportunity to confront survival and security issues. The first chakra holds our fears about money, survival and basic instincts. It reflects our overall sense of security in life. Last night in prepping for this upcoming week I came across a letter in the mail that stated our personal information had been compromised this week, and to cancel an account immediately. I know this can be common these days and felt two connection moments from it. First I flashed back to the dream from Chapter one of the nerdy computer geek who had my information. Now reading this letter I realized that I may have even seen exactly who committed this computer security breach in my dream! Although the accounts were fine when I checked on them, I could not help but smile that this was happening on the eve of the base chakra that deals with money issues directly.

What a great healing opportunity to get to the core of these fears by just facing them head on. I spent the next hour speaking to a few representatives on what our next steps were to protect this account. I affirmed that I was no victim here, and asked for clear guidance on exactly what to do next to secure all of our accounts. I stayed in gratitude for this advanced insight that I know was protecting me all along. I prayed for ongoing protection and to increase our consciousness to the point of no longer repeating or magnetizing this financial experience ever again.

Today is a day to wear vibrant candy red, and accent where you can with whatever level of color that feels appropriate. Great gemstones for this day are red jasper, garnet, red coral (I just received several coral pieces as a gift from St. Lucia yesterday!) Also ruby, cinnabar, or other red jewel tones work nicely. Bloodstone is another wonderful healing stone that helps to infuse a deep inner strength.

am journal: Another dream about leaving my purse while I was out of town. I then found my purse only to realize my wallet was gone? This dream topic being repeated has me checking every account and going through all of my records repeatedly. The thought then crossed my mind that perhaps I am going through an identity upgrade that is simply throwing out my old personal information symbolically more than literally. To then replace it of course with a new higher sense of self. I am praying this is more of a symbolic dream than literal.

Dressed playfully this am in a very festive, brilliant red Hawaiian sarong, also sporting red coral jewelry along with most of the stones mentioned above. Since the base chakra holds the element of earth, it is important today to get out into nature however you can to literally ground down. Even a patch of grass with your bare feet is enough to root down and experience mother earths loving support.

pm journal: Cranky! The weather was so cold and rainy out (needing lights on inside the whole day). Then my kids refused to go out on our walk. When looking at the bitter gloom outside, I couldn't blame them. I jumped on the rebounder instead and drank hot tea throughout the day to keep warm. I trust that this is perfect for whatever is integrating within. Yet honestly, I just felt distraught most of the day. I know it takes tremendous faith to pioneer any project that has not been done before in a certain way. I look forward to going underground tomorrow. Right now underground or at least under the covers to hide for a while, sounds good.

Day nine affirmations:

Today I connect to mother earth with my whole being.
I am fully supported by the earth
and give thanks for its abundance
I ground knowing that I am fully blessed
and held by the universe
Life supports every need on my path today
I am safe and secure in every breath

Day nine meditation prep:

1. What can I do to ground and connect to the earth today? (standing barefoot on the ground, laying down under trees looking up, laying on a bed of rocks)

2. What activities will support a better rooting here in my life today? (yoga outside with poses

like down dog and sitting forward leg stretch variations, time in nature, gardening, or pottery type crafting)

3. What red items can I use or add today to support the vibration of this chakra center? (red clothing, accents, any red flowers, drinking red juice beet vegetable juice is wonderful)

4. What can I do to feel better about my finances or personal security today? (call in guidance about your right steps (if any), or other needed changes, new financial plan)

5. What can I eat or supplement today to support this center? (beets, red apples, root vegetables, radishes, cinnamon, chili peppers, cayenne, tomatoes, red peppers, strawberries, cranberries, pomegranate, saffron)

Chapter Five
A day of Transition

Day ten

Day ten: below and at feet – (ground chakra) – brown – transition from body spiral to mind spiral - **Day of transition and grounding deeper in the earth to draw in earth essence and to remineralize within.**

Although this area can still have a first chakra feel to it, our ground chakra is where our feet meet the ground. I see this beginning just below the foot chakra on and below the ground. Light workers use this chakra in the earth to ground healing light into the planet. I was shown that this is an important day relevant here on this cleanse, for each of us to experience personally.

On this day of transition we flow just below the topsoil to a place of allowing whole support through being completely surrounded by the earth essence. Doing this allows the minerals within the earth to energetically regenerate us. Here we merge to gain strength from the roots of the earth while traveling from one spiral to the next. Today we are completing our ten day cycle of the physical. Tomorrow we will be entering into the spiral of the mind.

The blessing of this day is to root down even further than yesterday allowing ourselves to be enfolded like an embryo or a fresh seed germinating for new life. This cocooning is essential before going back up into the higher centers to engage the mind. Remember the power of your upper centers, depends on the stability and strength of your lower chakra centers. So please honor this day by being literally in the soil if you can. Grounding from yard work, planting trees, or even a good natural mud bath is highly recommended today.

Also take advantage if you live in an area near natural caves, or can go underwater to experience the ocean or lake floor (again going beneath sea level) while surrounded by minerals. The idea is to insulate ourselves and protect the changes we have just experienced, while charging up and fertilizing ourselves for the next phase. I have to admit yesterday was really challenging, for me personally. I felt unusually discouraged and prayed the whole day to just keep it together. So I welcome a day of ground support as I now glance down smiling at the sunshine pouring in next to me while I write this morning.

The color of today is brown or terra cotta like shades of earthy clay. Brown is a very nurturing shade, although I realize some people do not like this color. So if this does not feel right to you, go with black or warm grey tones instead. Any of these tones still represent the minerals in stones and basalt (black lava rock) still representing earth tones. A rich earthy brown represents the never ending roots of the aspen or mighty oak. As we engage this day of going within, it is important to hold firm intention to literally root deeper with our entire being.

Planting a tree or thick shrub can accompany a literal intention to ground deeper. Intend today to retract wisdom from your ancient connection within the earth. You can further open your own awareness about what the earth needs from us, once we are stable enough to give back. We can also share through its infinite wisdom, as we align our vibration with the ground. Whatever way you choose to celebrate this transition day is the right way for you. That may include more sleep, or other nurturing activities. It is also a day to finalize your physical foundation in order to move into the next phase of healing.

am journal: Dreamt I lost my car keys. I was trying to find my car to leave in the middle of the night, to get away from a strange factory I was working in. I was in a poorly lit parking lot very late, running around zig zagging through many cars when I finally found my own. I realized it was open and the keys were already in the ignition. As I jumped in the car someone loving and positive was right behind me. It was a weird sensation as I kind of sat on him (or we sat in the same seat at the same time), while I peeled out of this parking lot in a hurry. Turning onto the main road in a mad rush, I realized I had no idea where I was going, or where I was supposed to go. Then this man with me lovingly reassured me that "everything was just right."

Even after this unusual dream I still woke up oddly encouraged. Seeing the sun shine so bright earlier than usual, lifted me even more. I dressed in a long sleeve brown shirt and bright red fleece vest. Today I will carry black tourmaline, sandalwood, and danburite stones. Although it is still very chilly this morning, my kids and I are definitely going to venture out later today, cold or not.

Underground smoothie: banana, apricot, goji berry, coconut, cranberry, almond butter, raspberry, ginger, cinnamon, flax, hemp, oat milk, and colloidal silver.

My grandmother was a professional ceramist who taught for many years at the Norton Gallery of Art in West Palm Beach, Florida. So as a child I was blessed with being able to play with rich terra cotta clay daily. I was trained from a very young age alongside a master sculptor. Today just playing with my kids using simple model mix holds that same spirit of playing with the earth element. I painted earlier today with my children, and found myself drawing the same symbols I have been doodling for years now repeatedly. They seem to hold knowledge of their own that I can feel although interpreting this in linear form has still eluded me up to now. I am confident they will make sense one day. Sometimes we have to live our creations first. Only then in hindsight can we understand what was coming clearly. Or as the saying goes hindsight is 20/20.

With that in mind, let yourself doodle and express deep tones of your own inner knowledge that may swell from within you that are relevant for your own path. Play in the dirt today if you can, even potting a few flowers without gloves. Soil is healing. Rocks and roots hold immense intelligence that we can share when we respectfully approach them to experience their strength. Even sitting with your back to a large tree can teach you something if you are willing to feel it and listen. In working closely with the mineral kingdom I have been blessed with the gift of reading stones and crystals. Knowing what and where they work in the energetic system of another. I use this skill to help increase awareness about why others are each drawn to unique path stones that are indeed relevant for each person's soul purpose.

Rocks and soil when respected share infinite knowledge of the ages, and can hold frequencies for us that we might not otherwise maintain on our own. Part of my light work on the planet is helping to bring in and carry frequencies of balance and stabilizing support for the mineral kingdom. You may be one called into this work as well (whether you know it yet, or are awakening to this knowledge now). Heaven knows the more of us stepping forth to hold restorative frequencies for the planet, the better. I share this in hopes of inspiring you to volunteer your time and healing prayer for the earth today. While holding a vision that we may all combine our light and shine it into the planet to help regenerate her back into balance. This is possible.

As much as we can focus on the planetary damage (which I agree is relevant to acknowledge). Wouldn't our precious light and energy be better spent to expand a vision of healing (while taking action from this vision) to restore our planet to wholeness? Maintaining higher consciousness while living from this high space will create the frequencies of healing the earth needs. Use your energy to heal and move ahead and leave the drama and illusion of scarcity behind.

Day ten affirmations:

Today I root myself within mother earth
I keep a grounded foundation as I move forward
I transition well in life and flex with change easily
I embrace change and trust the blessings it brings
I ground light into the earth to stabilize
and heal the planet

Day ten meditation prep:

1. What can I do to experience the earth more today? (gardening, yard work, clay, mud bath, underground in any way)

2. Where can I go to be in the soil today? Or is resting and going within more appropriate? (time in the dark, out in quiet of nature, dark nap)

3. What brown or reddish earth tone items can I wear or use today to support this transition day? (clay, dyed organics in brown or red, or any items of earthy tones or if black, warm grey, also work as a

second choice)

4. What can I eat or supplement to support this transition? (tan oatmeal is wonderful for the nervous system, oat straw tea, also red beets, or any rooted veggies, reddish brown nuts or fruits are wonderful, amaranth, brown rice, or flax)

5. What else is appropriate for preparation going into the mental spiral? (drawing symbols using charcoal, clay, Zen sand drawing, drumming, journaling or any creative expression may help transition on many levels today).

Day eleven

Day eleven: base center – (1st chakra) – red – inbound mind spiral **- Reemerging into the first chakra to clear our perception of prosperity and personal identity**.

As we re-enter our base chakra today, the focus shifts from our last intention here. Experiencing the base chakra in the physical spiral was to confront our fear stored in our kidneys, bladder, and bloodstream. Now in the first chakra of the mind, we are facing our fears on the mental plane. Doing this serves to better clear our aura of old beliefs or negative affirmations we may still carry about our own level of personal security. As we move up and then down through our energy centers we will re-apply colors to the chakras as needed, yet on different planes in each spiral. Use as much as you are guided to in terms of food and other personal items, to support your own healing and growth in each center. If you know one chakra is of particular challenge, then it may be worthwhile to invest in a small extra item of support. Be creative as you find new ways to regenerate and develop each of your centers.

am journal: Slept awful last night. I heard noises all through the night. Even with intending to close my ear chakras more (to calm overactive clairaudience), movement and ongoing noise around the house still kept me up. I tossed and turned going over a million details of my schedule. Really if you think about it, our schedule is quite irrelevant when sleep is being lost over it. I prayed for the peace to surrender my overactive mind, until I finally drifted off in the wee hours.

am journal: Woke up late. Although I did not sleep last night, I feel fine and rearing to go. This morning I hold strong intention to choose joy no matter what life brings today. Obviously my initial dreams are pointing to classic first chakra challenge (of finance and security) which do not surprise me while I am doing my best to keep centered in a time of reasserting my stability in this center.

I feel the lesson in these issues and dreams (besides forgiveness), is to release our personal status to the universe, then trust the flow. Know that whatever you need will be there. Whatever is taken away is no longer serving you. As you work on this mental area energetically, the main objective is to stay out of victim mode in any chakra. Take full responsibility for everything you create, while trusting a divine outcome for everyone (which may or may not be to our egos liking). Our job in the first chakra is to keep our own gait steady, knowing that true abundance comes from our connection to the divine source of God, not any from any one business, client, or company.

This morning my children and I sat out in the yard under our grapefruit tree. My daughter sat and prayed for animals around the world, as she usually does. While my son went as high as he could climb into the upper limbs, attempting to pick the higher limb grapefruits (talk about deja vu). We then made some spelt, raspberry, and oat bran muffins. Keep reading about "getting happy." We all get to choose joy no matter what is going on around us. Sometimes this can be much easier said than done if we let our perception and thoughts drift toward discouragement or fear.

Dinner was a raw salad of freshly grated beets, daikon radish, cilantro, fresh lemon juice and a few raw olives. Even if it is a red fruit or accent within a meal you will still receive the benefit of this color. However root veggies like beets or radishes are especially grounding and nurturing for the blood and kidneys. There is something about the color red that does inspire and command attention. By just wearing a simple red t-shirt and a large red coral bracelet today, I felt a wonderful uplifting boost of stamina most of the day.

Day eleven affirmations:

I am stable and positive in every thought

I expand my financial vision today

I deserve infinite abundance

All of my needs are taken care of as I follow my path

The universe divinely brings forth everything I need in every moment

Day eleven meditation prep:

1. What old beliefs or affirmations can I release today to increase my personal sense of security and wellbeing? (releasing cords or beliefs that anything or anyone other than God/Spirit is the source of your abundance)

2. What can I organize financially to prepare for the future so I experience more peace and stability today? (reconciling your check book, checking current balances, seeking financial investment advisement if necessary)

3. How can I connect to an inner abundance wave that will create abundance from the inside out? (counting your blessings to find the infinite gifts and divine synchronicities that are within and surrounding us daily)

4. What can I share today to confirm my abundance and reflect faith that I truly have more than enough to give to others (or charitable causes) that I believe in? (sharing even a small amount is an action statement that you have more than enough in your own life)

5. What can I wear, eat, or accent with to support this bright red center today? (rooibos tea, cherry bark and red hibiscus teas are wonderful choices today, all red or root fruits and vegetables,

wearing bright poppy red)

Day twelve

Day twelve: sacral center – (2nd chakra) – orange – outbound mind spiral - **Recycling old ideas, beliefs that no longer support your path from your sacral center.**

Today we are venturing east into the second ring of the mind spiral. The sacral center correlates to the mental aspect of our boundaries with people, lifestyle and our creative energy. As well as the ability to assimilate whatever is going on in our life. The sacral center is going to address creation from where it originates. Everything we see around us from our jobs to our material items, were conceived of in some way within the mind, moving energetically through this center first. So today is an opportunity to delve into this chakra and clear out our internal creative clutter.

We do this by first taking complete responsibility for everything that we have created in the past. Next we move into present time, to focus with absolute clarity on what we desire to consciously create in our life now. This is really a fun chakra of rich emotion, vitality and sexuality. For those who are unstable and overly empathetic, this can be a nightmare when imbalanced. We all need proper boundaries to define why we are manifesting and co creating everything around us in life. Balance and strength here can help us stay on our own path instead of stepping into another's universe of creation. Winding onto another's path too far, can take us off of our own path.

Without ongoing self awareness of our channel we can get constantly distracted, or worse begin to follow someone else's goals, instead of our own. Without balance in your sacral center, you may also go unaware of processing others emotions. It is not uncommon to realize you may be using your own precious assimilation energy on others confusion. You may be helping others to assimilate their own life, yet this could be leaving you enzyme short for your own needs (emotionally or literally). I now understand that when I was a child, I had a tendency to take on others imbalances physically in this center. I pretty much had a phantom bloating belly ache off and on for years. If others came in high strung and anxious, I would suddenly go from calm to hyper in seconds. Now in hindsight, I understand I simply did not know any better.

Seeing the same clairsentient pattern in my own

children, I can now begin to train them to separate what is there own energy, as opposed to another's. Then more importantly, once we can discern what energy is not ours (to take on or hold), that we can then ground out the energy which is not our own.

I highly suspect that many ADD and ADHD children are in this same boat of absorbing everything around them to the point of ongoing overload. Many of these highly sensitive kids are growing up without the coping skills they need, leaving them in constant reaction to overload of too much negative stimuli around them. As parents we must first clear ourselves, and then hold a higher vibration to example a clear field for them. Our own healing can also heal our children simultaneously, while modeling better boundaries, clarity, and light for our children to follow.

It was not until my college years while living in Boulder, Colorado that I began to learn about alternative methods of living and being. This decade phase of awakening brought new skills and complex energy training from countless different teachers and resources. Although incredibly challenging to go within to heal core issues, it was priceless in helping me to reprogram my entire network. Now I have learned after two decades of tuning myself to a higher octave that this once "curse" of being so sensitive, has now become my greatest asset to be of service in the world.

Now I can smell trouble and people, and often know my purpose in various situations. I have learned to catch lower frequencies and unhealthy sensations from people I am in close proximity with, then reroute or transmute any lower energy before it has a chance to stick or alter my field. By catching energy on the outer fields first, this gives us the chance to remind ourselves quickly that a sudden pain, upset, or wave of depression (unbelievably common) may not be yours.

Perhaps it was someone you were standing behind in the grocery checkout line, right before a strange onset of anxiety or lethargy waved in. Yes, it is this ridiculously common and simple for sensitive people to blend with others around them. For me the second chakra was where I experienced the most challenge from this issue because of taking on others pain and constantly balancing the gap in overly submissive or aggressive environments.

Luckily in order to balance this as a child, I grew up near an organic orchard where I could hide in the safe haven of my grandmother's fruit trees. In the orchard with the nature spirits, I stabilized from day to day in the quiet citadel of the elementals domain. I literally came home from school and ran out barefoot to sit in silence for hours while eating tons of wild tangerines, tangelos, or star fruit. This divine gift balanced the chaos of my early life including many bizarre characters that came and went (who I now thank) for teaching me how to master these skills. Once I finally turned the table, committing to maintaining excellent boundaries, I regained my health and reversed most hypersensitive allergic responses altogether.

Today is a day to evaluate your beliefs and boundaries around who and what you are creating in your own life. Life belief statements such as "if it's not one thing then it's another," will gladly order pandemonium for you. Just this single belief statement alone (when believed) will indeed create one chaotic event after another. Not until we reclaim our spirit and release all victim mentality, can we release the illusion that we are at the negative mercy of anything. We always get to choose our emotions, no matter what is going on around us.

If we choose joy while madness parades on outside, then we are doing our part for inner peace. Better yet, imagine choosing the core belief that everyone and everything is aspiring to help us all achieve harmony, balance, abundance, and joy right this second. Through every breath we can unfold a whole new existence, as we weave a new reality together through this center from our own focused intention.

am journal: Up again in the night with many positive ideas whirling about....feel wonderful again this morning even with disrupted sleep. Today I am wearing a simple tangerine colored t-shirt, coral jacket with sunstone earrings. Made a hemp, coconut, peach, mango, banana, B-12, flax seed, goji berry, and wild dolphin essence elixir, with a little colloidal silver, smoothie which came out to a golden color with orange flecks in it. I feel the need to organize today and upgrade things around the house.

Go through your home with a simple good will bag can help to pick off excess items, so you can release them to a good cause. Try to find at least five old pieces today to share or release in the trash, to free up your own space up for a higher current. Although flow is important in every chakra, this is one center that when blocked, can constipate and hold in toxicity affecting the entire system.

Excess clutter around us can equate to blockages throughout our body. So watch where clutter is coming from, and ask yourself (if this room was an organ in my body which one would it be?) See if your inner response may reveal where an outward chaotic reflection, may be revealing an inner mess. Feng Shui (the art of energy placement) can also assist us here to line up colors and elements throughout the home. Even when we keep our personal space clear, it is still always good to do a regular walk through to see what you are ready to continually free up. Doing this helps us to maintain a high level of clarity. If you are not sure where to begin, just call in spirit to help lead you to what is right for you to let go of today. Or just ask, and see what pops into your head first. Is it a cluttered drawer? Could it be old books or photographs of old loser boy or girlfriends? Forgive them all, then rip them up and gladly throw them away? Anything small or large counts here.

In the beginning of the resource guide there is a fantastic second chakra soup called the Thailand rainbow nectar. I have made this today for lunch. It my own simple veggie variance on the traditional Tom Yum Kai coconut soup from Thailand. Like everything I share here, this is a flexible recipe (made to my preference) so if you like other root veggies, simply adjust it to your own liking.

Day twelve affirmations:

I create and honor firm boundaries
about what I am willing to think and create
I absorb and assimilate new ideas with ease
My mind now clears all blockages to
make room for new flow
I absorb and release everything in a balanced way
I release old mind sets keeping me out of greater flow

Day twelve meditation prep:

1. What do I need to absorb or assimilate to make progress in this center? (releasing and working with any area of procrastination, old unfinished projects, undeveloped ideas – let go or get moving)

2. Am I hoarding anything that is keeping me out of the higher flow today? (clothes not worn in years, outdated books, old keepsakes from negative relationships of any kind)

3. What would balance my sense of giving and receiving today? (where can I share, or what would I benefit from acquiring or receiving today)

4. What new concepts would I like to adopt into my life which I need to digest in order to integrate them? (journaling dreams, habits to be

released, exploring your divine soul purpose, sleep next to carnelian stone)

5. What can I accent with today to support this center mentally? (Orange foods, clothing, screen saver, get creative)

Chapter Six
Into the spiral of the mind

Day thirteen

Day thirteen: power center – (3rd chakra) - yellow – inbound mind spiral - **Clearing your power center in your home and work environment for greater mental clarity**.

A little higher now in the belly to evaluate power issues from a mental perspective. What do you believe you deserve in terms of power? Questions to consider here are who and or where we leak our power to? For some of us, this may be a slight power leak here and there, which is somewhat manageable. For others this might be a full aura sieve into a job or relationship that can exhaust our system (including adrenal exhaustion, or worse). If we are not careful here boundary damage can deplete our esteem and identity, while suffocating our inner fire.

The power center can be tricky as we

balance when and where to assert ourselves appropriately with confidence. When too much energy is asserted here we may find ourselves imposing our will (in a controlling fashion) on others. This only creates petty negative attachments from our solar plexus into theirs. Close your eyes and ask if you have any cords connected to anyone through this center right now? Don't be surprised if old relationships you thought were long gone are still hooked in here. If you can think of a past challenging person or situation without an emotional response (through either a sting or a pulling sensation) then you should be clear.

If there is an emotional swell within (or anxiety surfaces) then most likely there is a cord here from a negative power connection. Don't be surprised if you get an image of a co-worker you mentally spar with on a regular basis. If you are not forgiving anyone in your environment, or cringe in a way that contracts this upper abdominal area, you may need to address this issue. Releasing this connection can set you both free from the ongoing drain these cords can cause.

Remember to keep the willingness to forgive any person (or circumstance), while you calling your energy back from them. Just call in guidance from the highest healing light source that feels right for you. In some circumstances I ask the goddess Kali to help clear these cords. In other times I ask Christ, Archangel Michael, or another ascended master. These are just examples but call on what you feel spiritually aligned to which is a personal intuitive choice. Thank the lesson which you needed to learn, that corded you in the first place. When you free others to their own path, then begin to live by a higher energetic standard, this center will begin to remain clear. Soon you will know your own game, and catch yourself before you choose to engage in any such unhealthy energetic behavior.

am journal: For a few nights now I have heard popping noises and clunks coming from our garage in the middle of the night, even a few times during the day. At first I thought a squirrel must have crawled in there because the noises were so distinct. However as the week progressed I realized with a thud that we had "guests" in the garage. Finally on Friday, I planned to sage and clear this space along with my cleaning. First I grounded myself, and then continued through a simple process to assist clearing whoever was present.

As a tuned into what was going on I immediately began to connect the dots, realizing that as the week progressed; I began to only go in the garage when I absolutely had to. I was even going without tools and items needed just to avoid going in the garage at all. I simply kept my distance from this presence, even forgoing laundry (that had now piled up quite impressively). Finally now I was ready to see what was present there. Tuning in clairvoyantly I realized not one but two different entities were in our garage. I was shown two images that were both earthbound spirits. One spirit was a tall, intimidating, overweight, unhealthy looking male with a closely shaved head and a green and white thick striped polo type jersey (looked like an English rugby player) in the northeast corner. Then a gangly, frail, dark haired, thin, teenage girl (with bandages on her arms) was to my right. Her energy was so dense from manic depression that I quickly surmised this was why I was steering clear of the garage this whole week!

I was vigilant to stay in my own grounding, while calling in assistance to help these two transition home properly. The male immediately responded to this light coming in. He gladly released his form as he began to float up and rotate to the side. His form lightened and dissolved into a shimmering essence now eager to merge back to the light. I also realized from the visual (from his very distinct green and white striped soccer style, rugby shirt) that this same man was in my dream the night before. He was out in our street in front of our house, waving his arms trying to get my attention.

The young girl however, was not as eager to go. She began to tell me how her family had such a hard time after she passed, that she stayed here around them out of imprisoning guilt. Her energy was so dense to be next to, that I could sense this guilt as literal packs of punishing heavy weights all over her body. It felt like an underwater ocean weight suit meant to keep you down on the ocean floor. This is the only adequate description that could compare this feeling of being with her energetically. She also had an all-encompassing self hatred that kept her energy tight to her body like a thick layer of oil. I told her she did not belong here anymore, and to please trust this process. I assured her that God was waiting for her to cross home. She was terrified of making another mistake, and felt imprisoned here in a way that was really not helping anyone (least of all her).

It took several times of calling in everyone I could think of through her ancestral line since the first few prayers didn't budge her. I had to reach further, calling anyone and everyone that I had ever worked with on the other side. After a few minutes, the room was so full of such an indescribable light that I began to overwhelm from the surcharge and cry. The beauty of so much unconditional love extending towards this tortured soul was magnificent to witness. I watched as she finally slumped forward (surrendering the weights) and released her grip of the guilt that had held her captive here for so long. Her fragile underweight body dissolved into light as the angelic beings around her cocooned her body for safe passage home.

I collapsed crying and gasping for breath from this shift, which brought forth tremendous emotion in me of witnessing a soul in so much pain. I sobbed alone on the cold garage floor curling into a ball in front of my washing machine. As this shifted slowly, I basked in awe of the love around the room that encircled me from every direction. Afterwards I thanked all of the guides and angels for their assistance in this process. I then burned a sage cedar stick while leaving the garage door open for a while, to air everybody out literally! I also extended my boundaries of intention for other earth bounds to please not enter my personal space. Afterwards there was a normal lightness to the garage that matched the harmony chord of our home. Then I knew this process was complete and clear. I share this as an example of clearing work that can be done when we are stable, balanced and grounded.

Give yourself permission to feel healthy

power. Then safely use it in whatever way you are divinely led, in order to serve and heal the planet. Holding high esteem and integrity is healing for everyone. We serve no one by hiding or playing it small. No one is better off by being a 2 watt light bulb! We need to be our full brilliant selves. When we allow others the space to shine at some point they will return the favor (and reflection) back toward us. Once clear, you will be at a level of inner strength to better hear and go by your own pulse. Living at a high frequency is the place we can see and create miracles in. We are all capable of living our light to heal the world. Actually our collective light work is to live bright and clear, laughing our way through the dream.

Day thirteen affirmations:

I reclaim and balance my power today

I redefine my boundaries in life from full self esteem

I deserve respect from everyone and give it equally

I take responsibility for where my power has leaked

I live and love from full power without apology

Day thirteen meditation prep:

1. What can I do today to honestly evaluate where my power has gone? (watch your energy after talking to gossipy downer friends or relatives, evaluate what action is necessary to get your power back)

2. Who or what situation do I need to take my power back from? (does your job energize you or drain? friends? places you go?)

3. What can I do to create higher self esteem in my life today? (update your look, treat yourself to a spa day, upgrade something to honor your body or home more)

4. How can I honor others more so that my standard matches what I am expecting to receive from the universe? (build your strength, take what you give, share more)

5. What can I wear, eat, or indulge in today to support this center more? (Yellow flowers, big sunflowers are great, I reheated yesterday's Thai soup recipe adding golden beet shavings and ginger with lemongrass to power it up today, sun tan, camp fire, candle meditation)

Day fourteen

Day fourteen: heart center – (4th chakra) – green – inbound mind spiral - **Healing and releasing past heart center wounds.**

AAAAaaaaaahhhhOOOooommmmmmmmm. Let yourself try this a few times here to open and get into the warmth of your heart.

The only limit on what we can receive from the universe is where we stop allowing the flow in. That is a massive concept if you really stop to consider where (in any area of our lives) we put a cap on what is possible to have or experience with our family, friends, money, or time. As well as what level we choose to believe is really possible to receive or give from. Our heart is meant to open and share infinitely, which always comes back to fill us.

am journal: Went to the beach right away this morning. The brilliant greenish blue ocean was absolutely clear and the tide was almost all the way out. Decided to walk south this morning with several heart stones in hand, then guided to a small nautilus shell that had a wonderful energy and brought it along for the walk as well. I followed my usual body clearing routine while observing a few issues that had surfaced over the last few days. I asked to see the necessary intelligence, to learn more about what I needed to move through.

I was guided on how to proceed in this upcoming week. Since we are going into a deeper phase of this cleanse now, we may feel the need to rest more to allow our body and mind enough prana for deeper clearing. It's funny how we may lose perspective of our progress over time? As we take time to reflect back a few months or years, we may recall the contrast of how we used to believe or take care of ourselves, perhaps at a lower level than now.

Here getting a glimpse of your progress you can hopefully see how much you have improved over time. Instead of criticizing how you may not be perfect on this cleanse (or in life). We can choose to focus instead on where there is positive progress over time. I know keeping a heartfelt commitment on simple steps and modifications over time can eventually inspire you into a whole new way of being.

Saw a unique paradox today of my own past rhythm. There is a common misperception that by going faster on triple shot lattes and technological short cuts that we are getting more done in life. This is actually a false illusion, and can be injurious to us in the long run. If we slow and center ourselves enough to hold a clear outcome visual, and proceed only through right guided action, we can indeed become the turtle passing the frenzied rabbit. I was raised with the "go faster, work harder, hurry hurry" time belief and environment. This deeply ingrained pattern has been one of my greatest challenges to overcome (including releasing coffee, chronic busyness, and hurrying without even knowing why). These were simply habits of going non-stop that I chose to continue from my own parents and upbringing.

I now know this was not self-love. Self-love rests, paces oneself, and is enough in life without having to prove anything, or attain an absurdly robotic schedule. I know I am not alone in this heart issue (although it can really translate through any chakra). In the mind to heart connection this addresses the development of enough self-love to honor all of our needs. Love allows adequate time for our body, home, family and world. We must shift out of auto pilot to clear the mind. We need to live more intuitively in the present, only working hard as it feels divinely guided. Instead of thrusting forward to "be enough," is the discernment we can learn to act from.

pm journal: This may sound silly but I let myself

take a nap this afternoon, and I feel like I had a weekend getaway, (since this is such a rare indulgence for me). Although this may seem silly, it was a major step for me to say "I am going to LET MYSELF REST." Letting yourself live in your own natural rhythm, is the end result of self-love. For you this may not be a nap, but something else you know you need for your own equilibrium. Give yourself permission to have whatever it is that you need and want in your life. When we are full within we can then turn and pour our love and example of wholeness onto others.

Today was spectacular. Within the last few minutes of my walk along the beach, a dolphin swam up to bid hello. Once the dolphin moved on, I was guided to perform a beach labyrinth in the sand. I set intention to release heart issues still bothering my mind. I knew it was time to reprogram here, and wanted to stimulate my thymus more too. The thymus chakra is turquoise colored and sits between the heart and throat centers. As we bring the thymus center (on heart or throat area days) to a higher functioning level of immunity, this can activate higher vitality for us.

I began to drag my foot while hopping backwards pressing down into the sand drawing out an enormous spiral. After preparing the shape I placed a purple and green fluorite heart at the center. Next I placed a single chrysoprase stone at every other ring. I also added a moss agate on one ring, and piece of malachite on the other. Remember there is no one way to do this. You may want to use flowers, candles, or anything in the order you are guided to fit your needs. I just share my own labyrinth set up to illustrate a few creative examples for inspiration.

I noticed others watching me (out of my peripheral vision) wondering what I was up to. To be honest, I had to pee so bad by the end of my beach walk that this may have been the fastest (semi hopping) labyrinth ever performed. As I walked towards the center I felt pulled to the side very strongly towards the center (strong pull on the skull) from the vortex in the center. I continued paying attention with gratitude while circling back out. Once finished, I collected my stones and realized I had nothing to give as an offering to the beach. Leaving a gift is meant to thank the earth for its blessings added to your ritual. I looked down and saw the beautiful nautilus that I was really hoping to take home with me. Instead I buried it at the furthest outer point of the last ring. I covered it in sand with my blessings and thanks to the Goddesses and Mother Earth to now close this ceremony. I then hopped home to pee!

Day fourteen affirmations:

Today I give myself unconditional self love

My inner peace radiates out healing to the world

I love life and my place in it

I am free to breathe and take in life

I am open to receive and share my best in life

Day fourteen meditation prep:

1. What can I do today to nurture my heart space and open fully within? (deep in nature, meditation outside, herbal bath, heart labyrinth outside)

2. What can I forgive more today to be completely carefree within? (journal release of old hurts, thought systems you no longer want to use in life, forgiveness letters)

3. What extra green can I eat today? (Kale, fresh sunflower sprouts, seaweed salad, all green fruits and veggies (celery is excellent) are all very balancing to the entire system)

4. What can I accent with today to stimulate this center? (gardening is excellent, buying a simple houseplant, or any green stone or item you feel drawn to)

5. What can I let myself indulge in today to express self love? (anonymous gift, sharing)

Chapter Seven
Into the Core

Day fifteen

Day fifteen: throat center – (5th chakra) – sky blue – core of program - center of mind spiral - **Clarifying throat chakra needs and goals on your life path through honest expression**.

Today is approaching the core of the mind spiral. The placement of this chakra is truly fitting since the throat seems to be a national challenge for so many who do not speak their own truth (much less live it). Many of us slip into everyone else's agenda, sometimes going decades without ever connecting to our own inner nature. It takes work to really understand then creatively express our own true self. If we don't do our own soul work, our throat can deplete life force energy often wasted with meaningless social agenda or relationships not aligned to our higher path.

am journal: Up again in the middle of the night. A little cranky this morning and guided again (as I was on the last fifth center day) to be quiet and listen. Went to the beach early only to turn around before crossing the bridge to go back home. I chose instead to just lie still on the ground out in my garden. Don't want to do anything today. Realized this is the half way point of the thirty day period and the middle of this second spiral.

Going into the mind is definitely requiring an increased stillness. Perhaps I am better at the physical going and moving phase. Regardless, I am determined to stick with this focused intention to attune my mind higher. Although I assumed this throat day would switch to an outward expression, an inner silence still feels like my priority. For you perhaps an outward bold day of singing, toning, or joyous expression may be your appropriate experience. Follow whatever direction is right for you to give or listen to.

I sat out in the garden with large kyanite, and several blue lace agate pieces. These beautiful soft light blue stones are calming yet immense in their own vibrational make up. Since kyanite is useful in both the fifth and sixth chakras, I will continue with it for the next few days. I find kyanite holds and clears the air element well, allowing one to go into high spaces (to clear out and attune higher). Both of these are excellent stones to "air out" the throat and mind. The air element can be called on to create a clearing movement through the entire system, but is especially useful from the heart chakra up.

I have to admit being still for so long is not my forte. It is important to remember that silence is necessary to ground and create a new mental foundation. We all can use a break from the mass mind thought system taunting us to go faster, in order to seemingly accomplish more. Is this comfortable right now? No. Will it get easier? I believe so. So just laugh, unwind, breathe and relax.

Day fifteen affirmations:

I listen within and know *my* truth today

I express myself enthusiastically today

I voice myself where I need to (or stay wisely in silence)

I laugh and share life with honesty and joy today

I give myself permission to sound my healing soul note

Day fifteen meditation prep:

1. What do I need to express today to activate this area? (is there someone, or a situation I need to address or clear the air with)

2. What activity feels healing today?

(singing, painting, writing, toning)

3. Does a period of silence (or the whole day) feel right to me? (listening more, calming this area, fasting from words, letting this chakra recharge from the mind)

4. What therapy would help this area today? (ear candling, neck massage, dry brushing skin in lymph area, sound healing is excellent through the entire chakra system)

5. What can I eat, wear, or accent with to assist healing today? (blueberry smoothie, lavender or thyme tea, raw honey (soothe throat) Wearing topaz/sky blue, or denim blue is great.

Day sixteen

Day sixteen: third eye center – (6th chakra) – cobalt blue – outbound mind spiral - **Third eye chakra clearing old records, updating personal information for greater peace of mind**.

Today begins the outward turn from within the core. We now step into the rich indigo blue (at the center of the mind chart) to journey back outward in a counter-clockwise direction. This is symbolic of reentering our mental existence here with a clean slate. This day can be a turnabout and a real shift for you in a positive way if you have been holding firm intentions while following through to free yourself from the old. When we release what is no longer working in our mental plane, then open to higher patterns of thought process, this can lead to inspired living in every aspect of life. This is a good day to start fresh. Also a great time to get rid of old phone books, journals, even old music, movies, etc. that may not be expressing your highest thought level any more.

I have come across old music this morning that I used to think was moody and introspective. Now it sounds just plain depressing, even silly that I ever chose such brooding lyrics. Old music or items may reflect old unhappy relationships, or times of unhealthy dramatic challenge in your life. You may benefit from liberating yourself from these today (if you feel ready). Now I see many of my old cd's are expressing a victim tone that I no longer want to participate with, and feel ready to release fully. I can now see many items and choices of entertainment through music and video were never supporting me at a high level. If this resonates with you, then it is an important step to evaluate by going through your personal items. Unhealthy negative drama can be easily found in music, television, basically all input from our environment. Ask yourself what personal items support your highest expression of light? Then ask if there is anything you would benefit from releasing to achieve your own highest vision of being?

Think of this step as releasing an internal layer from within the mind. Now entering week three here, I am definitely releasing old internal layers. For me this is being experienced in weird ways mentally as old situations and thoughts resurface in passing, while simultaneously being purged physically. You too may find that old negative patterns and pessimistic worries that you have long since left behind, can get stirred up and reengaged while cleansing. Cleansing can feel temporarily vulnerable as old images and dense forms kick up into the bloodstream to be released for good. Trust that any old visions, feelings or patterns repeating now will pass soon.

The last few days have been very challenging for me. Today I finally feel as though I am lifting out of this funk. This is not the time to give up. Although yesterday I admit to wondering if I had enough stamina to keep going another two weeks. This morning I have renewed strength that I will succeed, and all of this effort will be worth it. That is the trust involved in cleansing. Not everyone can afford to go get before and after diagnostics to prove their own internal progress. Although I have done that in the past and found it to be a great confirmation that you are indeed improving (in blood quality or hormonal balance). Otherwise we must trust our progress and enjoy the benefits we can see. These may include clearer skin, improved memory, or increased energy (to just name a few of the infinite benefits).

We may never realize all of the multidimensional benefits of cleansing. There are so many great books out there on this topic that I will not go into great detail here. Only to mention that when you do release old layers within the body, you greatly increase your absorption ability (to increase the percentage of nutrients you will assimilate) from your food and supplements. The cleansing process keeps your body functioning at a higher level of immunity, which is critical in this day and age. Even those committed to a healthy lifestyle can still benefit from regular cleansing.

Have you ever noticed the twisted hands of arthritic conditions, excessive cellulite, or general weakness "claimed" to be aging? This can also be an accumulation of toxic material deposited in the joints and fat tissues. When we make an educated effort to clear out this old material on every level, we increase the life force throughout our whole system. This can also increase our chances to avoid chronic issues later. It is possible to release pain now and in the future from this process. Cleansing is taking responsibility for your body and mind, instead of being at the mercy of any supposed statistic.

Preventative care is everyone's personal responsibility, and the key to helping us stay out of the victim mode in regards to disease. At this level of awareness we can participate consciously with every process and rhythm of our own physical body. This cleanse is an awakening into a higher attunement to your own biorhythm and natural cycles. It is meant to help remove old patterns keeping you out of your life's purpose here, while getting you into greater personal flow. This does not mean disease will always be absent. Sometimes we learn incredible lessons from illness. Preventative care simply manages our whole self to the best of our ability to minimize disease wherever possible.

Taking responsibility for our thoughts and perceptions is a necessary effort to evaluate our progress. Are we processing life at a high level? Or simply playing constant catch up while feeling victim to our circumstances? Do you feel in control or constantly on the offense? Are you happy with what your overall thoughts are creating in life? These are important questions to consider on our inner quest to maintaining wholeness and proper health of the third eye center. If we ignore our soul path hiding in dead end jobs and relationships, this may one day bring an ugly wake up call. If we are way too open, trying to anticipate every incoming nuance, this third eye area can become overwhelmed. Akin to the game frogger, we can experience the little frog anxiously trying to cross the road through rush hour traffic. The imbalanced third eye becomes the frog crossing the highway with too much input whizzing from every direction, keeping us confused and off track.

Balance here today is found by being very honest and open about your mental investments and what they are reaping. If you find that your relationships and or work are not giving healthy dividends in return for your efforts, it may be time to get frank about the truth. Then decide to reclaim your mind by changing it for the better. Take time meditating about what action, if any, is right for you at this time. Or if you are in a good situations in work and home then ask what you could do to refine this area to increase your personal flow even more. Finding where you need to clarify in this center is the goal today.

Day sixteen affirmations:

I release old thought forms and concepts
that no longer serve my life
Today I evaluate where I invest my mental energy
I only focus on people and places
that heal and increase my energy
My third eye is cleansed and open today
I do not hesitate to release old business
or personal clutter today

Day sixteen meditation and prep:

1. How will I make time today to evaluate the people, work and mental investments that I have chosen up to now? (meditation, personal records, or journal time to be honest about where you are in life)

2. What can I do today to organize and increase my peace of mind and inner strength? (organizing office material, catching up on projects or releasing old unfinished work, releasing old books, music, etc)

3. What can I do to relax and nurture the mind today? (organic facial, ear candling, pancha karma (third eye treatment), scalp massage, washing hair, toning mantras)

4. What can I supplement today to relax the mind? (chamomile, lavender tea, skullcap, oatmeal, magnesium, calcium, omega oils calm the nervous system and sooth scattered thinkers)

5. What indigo items can I accent with today to assist my process today? (purple tanzanite, amethyst, violets, kyanite, lapis lazuli, sodalite, dark red grapes, plums, indigo clothing, flowers, jewelry etc)

Day seventeen

Day seventeen: crown center – (7th chakra) – violet – outbound mind spiral - **Integrating scattered thought and belief fragments back into the crown chakra**.

Going up into the crown today and rounding the first loop out into the expanded mind. The crown chakra is a whitish lavender violet that opens to the sky and connects us to our guides, or other higher divine forms of communication. Too often people lose sight of their path and blend into someone else's agenda, while this centers guidance and support goes ignored. The crown center floats a few inches above your head connecting you to divine truth. Your soul work may or may not coincide with your own personal agenda (depending on our level of ego's involvement). If we are balanced and open, a non logical direction for the day may surge forth. So be sure to stay on track with whatever rhythm or spontaneous direction speaks to you.

An inside lead from the crown chakra requesting you to drop everything to go check on another person or place, may be your highest (divine) work for the day. Some of us may not acknowledge our internal guidance. Others may shoo inner whispers away, with a never ending "after I finish my own to do list," in response to spirit. When we take time each morning to get our inner directives first, we will be guided to our higher priorities. This can take courage to follow and live.

am journal: finally I slept. Thank you angels! Wow I feel so much better today. My cleanse is going well, and the changes have been comfortable for the most part. Wonderful meditation last night with a celestite stone. Celestite feels wonderful and helps to transmute lower worries into light. It also helps to eliminate negativity, and can help you to focus on gifts of the divine instead of ego concern. This makes it a wonderful stone for the 6th, 7th, and 8th chakra to help align higher fields and integrate light from them to hold and live by.

If you happen to be given a gift of any stone (that you feel good about), know that this is a gift from the universe to support you from the mineral realm. I have a tremendous affinity for this kingdom and work with it daily holding and sharing frequencies to support the planet. Actually we all are working with some family whether it is the animal kingdom, mineral, or other elements. The fun begins when we become consciously active supporting these kingdoms. You can feel whether you work with one, or all of these families. Our planet needs every one of us helping and healing our part of the whole. Work where your affinity is and you will be led to your earth healing work.

This is why balance and integration of the whole system is necessary. Being a competent human and a highly attuned functioning spirit are required for true success on your path. If we get too caught up in the daily grind and miss our calling, we may keep our bills paid on time, but still can miss the boat for our soul mission here. At the other end of the spectrum, if we go off into airy fairy doodle all day world, we can let our physical self go. Here we can a-wall responsibilities and not follow through in practical matters still relevant on our path. Flaking out all over the place does more harm than good, even if we are chatting with higher realms. Balance and true power comes from being responsible, taking care of our whole self, while fully connecting at high speed to our guides and core universal connection. This is the formula for wholeness.

pm journal: Went to see acupuncturist today to help assist cleansing. While she was putting needles in to strengthen several areas for me, I asked about acupuncture being used for opening the chakras. I shared this project, and that today was my crown chakra day. I was not sure what to "do" besides active meditation. She then added several cranium points with to my treatment. Immediately my head began to swirl while squeezing sensations shifted all over my skull. She then showed me a qui gong breath to pull higher chi through the whole system. Finally she added a chakra drumming cd for the crown center section (which I smiled at, since I had this same cd at home) to help this process.

Even the first breath of this treatment brought forth strong visuals of what was happening within. I then saw and heard that this first chakra burning in my bladder was my holding in and trying to control incoming information from spirit. I should instead open more and release fear about being supported on my spiritual path. Ouch. I listened and observed as this trance like state began to swirl clockwise then counter clockwise in several directions as this crown area was gently tuned up.

I quietly observed within my body as the swirling grey particles in the first chakra begin to lighten after about five minutes. Then they began to spin in an even pattern instead of whirling sporadically (as they did in the beginning). Back up into the crown, I watched as the patterns went up and out in an upward directed funnel. Then they shifted into a sideways and zig zag heart monitor like wave that went round and round the crown area instead of up and down. This continued on for a while and when I opened my eyes they began to tear like crazy. I have always suspected this means a very high frequency helper or two was with me.

I began to run reiki energy and saw symbols come forth in silver, white, then translucent clear watery luminescent shades. After the session was finished I went home to walk in order to better assimilate this input (or to ground back down). It is so important to take your time to ground well after this type of work. You can do this by eating, bathing, or sitting on the ground outside following any deep mediation. This allows you to use this energy by grounding it back into the physical plane instead of just playing in the sky without rooting the frequencies in a practical manner to be manifested and supplemented here.

Day seventeen affirmations:

Today I connect to my guides and angels with ease

I now release anything keeping me out of higher communication

I am willing to know and follow my truth today

I clear my connection to the divine today

I trust the universe and follow my inner guidance

Day seventeen affirmations and prep:

1. What can I do today to increase my connection to source? (increase quiet time, less or no TV, be in nature, meditation)

2. What can I do to clear this chakra today? (try tuning forks to clear the higher chakras which help to calm and attune, sunlight, fresh ocean water can clear with its strong ions, spraying rose water in the crown)

3. What guidance have I known for a while but have not wanted to acknowledge? (have you been guided to move, help someone, leave or improve an important personal situation?)

4. How can I create a stronger spiritual discipline? (prioritizing meditation and morning prayer, spiritual trips, daily reading, classes)

5. What can I eat, wear, or accent with to assist this process today? (blueberry, white and lavender items or foods, skullcap tincture, white tea, or fasting today if appropriate, praying over water infusing healing symbols See Dr Emoto's book 'Messages from Water')

Chapter Eight

Going Astral

Day eighteen

Day eighteen: sun center – (8th chakra) – gold – outbound mind spiral - **Up into the eighth sun chakra to align with healing etheric essence**.

I love the sun. Our sun chakra is above the crown, although some find this center also holds moon and other celestial energies as well. You decide what resonates more for you. This is the center of sun essence and healing light that we can use throughout our system. When this light is brought into the body during a healing it can clear and regulate the body centers quickly. I see this chakra working in and outside of the body as an adaptagen, to revitalize and adjust as needed where ever it travels. I use it to upgrade the entire system for myself and others. The sun chakra essence can also be seen as a sparkler like, going through the centers sparking and igniting the system with its brilliance and perfect golden white essence.

Remember when going up into the crown or sun chakra that further up and out is not necessarily better. Traveling astrally to run with our spirit totems can be exhilarating, but only if we come back and ground properly. Otherwise it is pointless to go up in the first place. Think of it like skydiving. If you are going to go skydiving you will prepare right? You put on your gear, goggles, and hopefully remember your parachute. Then after you are done with your exhilarating jumps, do just get in your car and drive home without taking off your goggles, or rolling up your parachute? Imagine getting home to fix dinner dragging a huge parachute in behind you. Obviously this is silly. Yet this ridiculous example is a relevant comparison with one important difference.

I mention this here because I have visited many spiritual gatherings of group that were all happy to shoot out of the body to explore higher realms, only to abruptly return and dismiss everyone without properly grounding the group back into their bodies. This incomplete practice left many scattered and vulnerable, not the best combo to then drive home. When you astral travel alone (or with a group) hopefully you prepare by protecting your field and creating sacred space around you. Then as you arrive back to present time, do you hop up and go about your business ungrounded and too loose energetically? This would be your parachute hanging out. For most of us this is harder to spot, since being ungrounded is invisible. Others may just report that you have become a flake or a space cadet. If we allow our life to become too scattered this can keep us off track and off path, which does not serve anyone. So pack up, and come back fully after playing in the sky.

I am incredibly grateful for the energetic tools and wisdom from countless teachers throughout my life. My training has kept my feet on the ground, while lifting me higher than I would have ever flown solo. I now finally understand what is going on when I am suddenly flooded with someone else's memories or pains which are not my own. I am grateful for the skills to clear space without drama or fuss. Exploring deep levels to discover new insight is important, but only when we can re-root down to properly integrate this higher light into our life.

A good way to know if you probably still need grounding is if you need everyone to repeat things over and over. This is usually what happens to me. Or if you can't find your personal items (keys, purse) when leaving a therapy session or group. Simply going outside to put your feet on the ground (preferably barefoot) can literally root you back down. Standing or sitting and rooting down through the soles of the feet into the earth can be very helpful to reset the body. This helps you to more fully reengage yourself into the moment of now. This also helps to anchor the insights and frequencies you journey for.

Yesterday I knew I was off balance while leaving the acupuncturists office after my treatment. I kept forgetting what I was going to say and then asked twice about my appointment time (major red flag hint to ground more). This is a typical example of when to acknowledge the need to re-center, in order to pivot and rejoin present time fully. Who can blame us when being out of the body feels so good? Yet nothing is accomplished well when we are not fully here. After a eating a snack and walking in the grass, I was back into my feet and ready to move on.

am journal: As much as I envisioned this day being supernatural and full of spiritually bliss, the truth is that I slept horrible. My son woke up and rolled out of bed in the middle of the night. So this morning feels less than enchanting. I went from cranking and grunting my good mornings, to glancing up at the bathroom mirror (not recognizing my squished eyes) while muttering "you have got to be kidding me."

It's funny how a "spiritual life" has this glamorous idealistic side projected onto it. Some may idealize a time when we will stay in nirvana, blissfully going about the day enlightening others while dressed from head to toe in flawless white, with soft soothing music in the background. However reality may pose the humor of large permanent stains on this white clothing, child rearing noises in general drowning out the soothing anything in the background. Not to mention insomnia, poopy diapers, and other life challenges that may gong our unrealistic expectation altogether. Only to shatter it into the perfect chaos we all find ourselves in. Every day we get to decide if we are going to have a good day or not, no matter what we are starting out with. Squishy eyed exhaustion or not, I am going to have a great day.

Perhaps what we need to release is the unrealistic high ideals any of us may set from time to time about what should be here, or not. Trust that everything with you is serving your higher good. You will be guided on the right changes to make. Otherwise everything is exactly as it should be. Allowing a greater connection to the divine will build a spiritual foundation that can help us to move into more of who we really are.

pm journal: Did my best today but caught myself going through the motions in mediation, work, and predictable chores, etc. Need to sleep better tonight. Everything just felt skewed, and I am avoiding everyone. I crave more than what is here in my universe at this time. Or so my ego whines. I know that spirit is where we are (no matter where we are). Yet today I honestly wanted to escape back in the mountains where I used to live in Colorado. In my meditation this morning, I traveled to the top of Bell rock in Sedona and stood on top of the south cliff looking outward admiring the ancient majestic terrain there.

After this meditation while going through the day, I felt jaded. Everything around me seemed dull. Now as I sit here writing slowly I find myself staring out wondering quietly "is this it?" This several year phase has been a period of observing life from within a fishbowl. After years of painting this still life theme of two or three fish swimming together within a vase, I now understand what I was expressing. I actually began to paint these the year prior to entering this "fishbowl phase," literally. I recall feeling apprehensive about what this art represented, only to experience it literally later within that same year. Over the years this has taught me to stay vigilant about anything I drew or painted, since my art animates to life quite literally.

The fishbowl phase has been one of constant silence and solitude. Life was blessed and simple in this phase of child rearing. I know many mothers can relate to this chapter of working, breastfeeding, and observing the world from a distance (while possibly feeling invisible within their own vase) watching others pass by. I now understand the symbolic truth from painting this image over and over again, both before and through this period. All the while questioning whether or not I was ever going to have natural space to swim, other than some oddly fitted tank?

My progression to healing was to build enough faith and stamina to allow full creative development from my own higher vision to manifestation. We all can do this regardless of where we are, no matter what we think we need. We all have to liberate our self in some way from the illusion of captivity. This is where the brilliance and perseverance qualities of the sun can keep us thriving anywhere. We must keep enough heat and inner strength to see our divine purpose through, no matter what our perception may be. In other words, shine on.

Day eighteen affirmations:

I accept the gifts of the sun into my being today

I call in light to heal and balance my entire system

I give thanks to the sun today for its infinite abundance

My spirit is illuminated by the sun today

The sun melts away anything that no longer serves me

Day eighteen meditation and prep:

1. When will I make time to be in the sun today? (dry UV sauna uses the good UV rays, also high quality sun lamps, or simply meditating in the sun can be helpful if in dark climate/winter)

2. How will I work the sun into a mediation that works for me today? (gratitude prayer to the sun, yoga poses with sun salutations, lunar yoga)

3. How much "live" food can I eat today to eat the rays of the sun? (live raw fruit, veggies, blue green algae, or sprouted greens all carry sunlight vibrations that ignite you internally)

4. What can I do to spread joy and cheer today and surprise others in a fun and clever way? (sharing in whatever way feels like a grand blessing to others, having a healthy gourmet party, beach or park picnic in the sun)

5. What can I accent with in gold, neon yellowish sun tones, or moonlight silver to help assist this process? (Sunstone, rainbow moonstone, gold, silver, platinum, wearing gold and silver shades, think royalty and upscale)

Day nineteen

Day nineteen: crown center – (7th chakra) – violet – outbound mind spiral - **Integrating higher mental clarity light and guidance into your crown**.

The outer loop of the mind spiral integrates an upgraded mental clarity today then completes tomorrow in the second transition day leading into the spiral of spirit. Having the crown twice in the mind spiral seemed odd to me, before I began the process myself. Yet as each day was revealed, I was shown why each curve and placement was indeed completely relevant. Every color and placement incorporates many levels of energetic exchange and harmonizing for your own journey.

I am also finding there are added surprises along the way for each of us. These synchronicities and gifts will unfold for you in an individually unique way to confirm that you are on your own individual right path. Learn to intuit and follow your own signs, while keeping track of your own highest path coming from your inner heart space.

The reason there are two crown days in this spiral is to allow increased support for our mind while attuning it to a higher frequency. It is important to remember that we are always aligned with spirit, but can increase this connection with conscious effort. Attuning higher will give us everything we need to know in every moment of our path. The mind spirals objective is to fully release everything we have erroneously chosen (or given) to think that no longer serves us. It also helps to release any beliefs that are creating limitation on our path. Anything impeding our growth must be cleared before we will have room to reprogram our mind with more empowering input. When we flush out our mind enough to stay in flow, then we can make great strides on our path. Clearing our metal garbage releases confusion and second guessing which is coming from our own self doubt mired by our very head clutter.

am journal: up 5:20am. Up most of the night with back pain. Wondering what I am holding back there? Could not get comfortable no matter which way I turned. Not sure what today brings? Being day nine of this second spiral, this is a closure (or forgiveness) day within the mind. Anything that feels incomplete for you would be beneficial to find closure with today. Keep reading about self-reliance over the last few days. Seeing many small yet distinct trail crumbs of needing to forgive myself, and be at peace more.

Today is overcast and chilly. Funny just as I wrote this, the sun burst through my window with a strong beam. This is a great day for tai chi, yoga, water therapies, and high altitude climbs. Wind can assist us today, to shift our direction if we are off track. We also must secure our grounding so we don't blow away like a kite off its string. When aligned properly here, we can increase our velocity to transform and accelerate with ease and grace more than ever before. There is nothing like fresh wind in your sails.

Day nineteen affirmations:
Anything not part of my higher path
is now released into the wind
I love working with higher frequency guidance
Life supports me with infinite resources
My mind and path are divinely directed
I inhale support and am guided along easily

Day nineteen meditation and prep:

1. What loose ends or old patterns in the mind can I complete now? (writing a completion letter, releasing old items, forgiveness ceremony, releasing unhealthy contracts with others)

2. What can I call or do today to create closure for the mental phase? (complete outstanding forgiveness calls, sending love wherever you have withheld it, sharing as guided)

3. Is there anywhere I should visit or go to help accomplish this today? (ocean, park, place you have been avoiding but need closure at)

4. What can I do to nurture this area today? (Head massage, washing hair, head stand yoga poses (if at this level), toning)

5. What can I eat, wear, or accent with in lavender to whitish tones to help assist this process? (skullcap, chamomile, celestite, amethyst, spirit quartz, violet orchids,)

Day twenty

Day twenty: ground center – (ground chakra) – brown/black – transition day from mind to spirit spiral - **Grounding light into the earth to support transition from mind to spirit.**

Today is our final transition day going from the mind spiral into the spirit realm. Tomorrow marks three weeks on this cleanse which is a wonderful accomplishment. Although it is nice to glance off the side of the mountain for a peek at your horizon, there is still a ways to go to complete this final upward spiral.

This brown day calls us back underground to drain our excess into the earth. As I mentioned before going to sea level or below it (if possible) would be great. If this is not possible then just lie on the ground outside where ever you are. Here you can venture into the realm of spirit, while sinking within the soil for support. Today is a great time to sweat (dry uv sauna is wonderful). Or to get dirty in the yard, repot plants, or pull weeds. If you are up for it, try a hot Kripalu yoga class to sweat (at 108 degrees) while reaching deep flexibility both physically and mentally.

Earthly support is needed to align our

system with natural forces to protect our transition. Today I am wearing a simple brown t-shirt, and plan to catch up on a lot of yard work that is long overdue. I actually look forward to trimming and planting several indoor potted palms that are more than ready to get outdoors. I also have an acupuncture treatment scheduled this afternoon to help prepare for this final phase.

am journal: Slept well last night. I was already in the third eye mode this morning while going through my morning prayer, when I remembered this was the brown transition day. I went back through my notes and a forward review of the spiral (to again question my original intuitive mapping route). While tuning in, I asked my guides why I felt a third eye pull this morning? I was shown that the map was correct, and guided to trust it. Today's objective is to consciously reset the entire system. As we deepen our roots while taking a grounding breath, we set our intentions from a deeper solid core into this final spiral of spirit. This will achieve better long term results from setting at the earth level first before going back into the sky (or air realm). I walked through several other variations of this final spiral and realized the initial information from spirit was (duh, of course) the right formula. I was encouraged to stop thinking through this process altogether. Everything will make more sense once the entire quest is complete.

Today I am wearing brown and dark olive green, while carrying a large rough piece of tangerine quartz to help connect down. My cleanse is going very well, and deep layers are definitely clearing out. I am not sure what lies ahead in this final spiral. Actually I have not known much until each day happens, which is usually a good sign that you are in the flow. In the theme of underground today think of dry or warming combinations to help cocoon yourself. Hot chai or spicy Aryuvedic kapha herbal tea is great since it contains all of the wonderful warming spices like cinnamon, clove, and fresh ginger. All root vegetables or ground fruits will also support this energy. Soups, hot tea, and most spiced Indian, Thai and so on, are all wonderful choices today. If you can get in a mud bath, dry brush your skin, or induce sweating, this will also intensify purification to release toxins through the skin.

Although today may have a slow motion feel to it, realize that you are actually going a great distance (as well as through the sacred God/Goddess center) while being as still as possible. First we leave the mind going out into the unknown, to then enter the final spiral of spirit. Humanity is collectively entering the spiral of spirit now. The sooner we all awaken and balance here, the better. Why? It is crucial now because as we align and unite in a higher perspective of the universe, we will finally stop destroying it. We will instead seek the wisdom to regenerate our planet when we realize that as we breathe the earth breathes. As the eagle soars, we soar. We are all one. When we really access this and live it, we will stop the madness, as we release all illusion of separation. As we awaken and accelerate this consciousness, we can change the outcome of the planet.

As we approach this final spiral, please acknowledge how much work you have done so far. Give thanks to the many spirits, guides, angels, elementals, and ancestors who are cheering you on from the other side in every moment. Our ancestors and guides both present and seemingly absent are all worth remembering and honoring today.

Today is a day of death. A time for us to metaphorically decompose, to watch the old layers of ourselves fall away back to the mother earth. Only then can we reabsorb this energy, to rebirth into a higher elevation of spirit. This is a day to go under the surface fearlessly. Knowing everything seemingly good and bad is still only energy that will continue to change form endlessly.

While doing chores today I got into a deep space of this understanding. I saw a draining and absorbing happening from the ground. Similar to when a carcass if left to rot and simply drains back into the earth, reabsorbing at a cellular level into the soil. We too need to let our old self drain out, to then reabsorb fresh minerals. This will help us to gain new visions in rebirth, which the third eye will reveal tomorrow. As we blindly wander through our cave today in the dark, we need to get through our own channel of incomplete. When we reach the final spiral tonight in our sleep, we can intend to rebirth into a higher level of light with the fresh dawn.

pm journal: Acupuncture was incredible. What a divine blessing this new relationship has brought to help assist such accelerated growth. I am really grateful for such assistance from this ancient sage. Explained to her that today was my "underground" day. Felt the need to drain and clear my entire system to clear any incomplete work. She completely understood and did several points to help draw out this flow through my feet. Once she left I went into a spontaneous vision of going into a dimly lit deep cavern. I saw a multi colored crystal wall with water flowing through the luminescent sheer face, flowing gently down shifting the shades of the colors all over the face of the rock. The immensely pungent smell carried an earthy, musty, odor rising from underground supporting my being.

I laid flat and watched my surroundings as I began to experience myself melting into the black soil floor of this cave. I saw a counter clockwise spiral larger than my head spinning over my entire field that worked its way down underneath my entire system and flushed out under the feet. I wanted to get active in this meditation but kept being told to "just stay still," to allow this healing shift.

After a few minutes, painful fragmented memories surfaced of old fine art projects, business ideas, friendships, charity projects, and past creative writing pieces, that all needed to flush out from my inner core into the ground below. This surged forth with strikes and sharp pangs of anger, frustration and intense grief. Especially when so many of these projects were made from such positive expectations and focus. Yet I knew that in order to make room for the new, these old and incomplete fragments had to go. I saw visually that my second chakra had a small portion that was not igniting in my regular meditations. I suspected this was physical as well as emotional. So this was also a focus in this acupuncture session. I intended to add voltage into this area in order to get the lights back on here. When complete I could see a faint light in this quadrant had improved what was dark before.

Afterwards I went on to a crystal store along Indian Rocks Beach, to say hello to some taller than me natural cave figurines of amethyst. As well as some life size Tibetan statues that were truly awe inspiring. "Drain.... drain" I thought to myself as I wondered through this breathtaking store. I was open to support from this treasure haven, filled with hundreds of charged crystals and gemstones from around the world. I chose a large rough rose quartz to add to my home. I was also drawn to purchase red garnet, and small carved wooden statue of Kuan Yin to add to my prayer alter.

Day twenty affirmations:
Today I go underground to root and drain
I allow nature to support me and absorb its wisdom
I engage my earthy side and align to my deeper roots
I spend time outdoors today to transform the old
I am attuned to the cycles of nature with ease

Day twenty meditation and prep:

1. What can I do to get earthy today? (potting plants, weeding, playing with clay, mud bath, underground meditative journey, shamanic work, drumming)

2. Where will I spend time outside to make the most of this day? (visit a great park, garden, local nursery, caves)

3. What practical ways can I experience this if I am in a city or not close to a park or garden? (cooking with your hands, or even time in a health food store inspecting rooted veggies still allows one to hold and experience this root vibration, make a stew, or fresh raw salad)

4. What can I eat today to root more? (All rooted veggies, daikon, radishes, carrots, ginger, sweet potatoes, mineral supplements ground us to the inner earth)

5. What can I wear or accent with to help this process today? (brown, earth tones, amber, sandalwood, woodcarving, sculpting clay,)

Chapter Nine

Engaging the spirit

Day twenty one

Day twenty one: third eye center – (6th chakra) – cobalt blue – inbound spirit spiral – **Opening the third eye chakra to clear the senses for greater personal attunement and awareness**.

This may seem an odd radical shift going from the transition underground day, then right into the third eye. Yet after a solid day of grounding into this final spiral we can now open our vision further, using our newly reinforced foundation to hold higher frequencies more consistently. Today can be a wonderful day of opening and revelation for some. For others there may still be work to do here, to continue clearing out old limiting beliefs. So you can then expand to what is possible within this realm.

am journal: Appointment this morning for a uv sauna to further clear from yesterday. Guided to bring my new garnet, amethyst and new toning bowl cd.

Once relaxing in the sauna, I realized (with only five minutes left), that I had not really started sweating yet. No sweat while sitting in 130 degrees for 35 minutes? After my sauna time was up, a woman peeked in and asked me how I liked it? I shared that I remember sweating so much last time, yet today I barely sweat at all. She let me know this was a good sign that my toxic load was lower than before. There was less to expel (since this type of sauna creates a higher quality sweat), and not just a dehydrating regular sauna sweat. This was a nice confirmation to hear. Especially when it confirmed that I had lowered my level of toxic material to a clear state. I knew instantly when I looked into her eyes, that we were supposed to exchange more information.

She then introduced herself as a therapist at this clinic who worked in many different modalities. I smiled realizing that she was going to do an initiation for me, into this final spirit cycle today. I asked what her schedule looked like in the afternoon, and she found she had one late space open. This just happened to be the only time I could be there too.

When I went back for the session I was excited and ready to work. I brought several stones with me, and was guided to bring my new toning cd. I asked her to play it during the session which she agreed to use. What started as a craniosacral session became a free form flow unlike anything I had ever experienced before.

To begin, she chimed a large crystal toning bowl which sent waves through me in many directions simultaneously. I saw this light in kaleidoscope like patterns of triangle shaped stars that expanded, then opened, and then turned inside out in slow motion. These lines then shifted into a paisley like shape that began to spin clockwise. Next these lines separated, opening the space in between each piece of each symbol as though they were being shattered in slow motion.

Towards the end of the session she put one of her own crystals into each of my hands. This immediately sent me spinning forward when I saw myself abruptly submerge underwater. Suddenly I was swimming at a furious pace under a brilliant green ocean surging at a speed that was incredibly intimidating. I clamored to adapt to this quickening sensation, trying not to hold my breath from this explosive expansion. I asked to see what was happening, and realized I was swimming with a small pod of dolphins under a brilliant emerald sea. I then began to feel guttural squeaks and high pitched signals come up so strongly within my chest to the point where I was either going to start high pitched squealing or laughing hysterically. This exuberance and lighthearted energy coming from the inside out was almost too much for me to contain. I also did not want to freak her out, or break glass in the room from a high pitched call (that was a semi-joke).

So I just sputtered here and there and giggled to myself, as I flipped and threw my tail about in a thunderous show off style. Then the light shifted as I shot down into an underwater tunnel that opened into an Atlantian cave like structure. Here I surfaced to see a woman with funky platinum blond hair drawing out graphic symbol codes or equations of some sort, onto a large wall in front of her. Many people were waiting silently in the background for her help. She then held a focused glance in this dolphins (my eyes were seeing through this dolphins eyes) direction and could exchange information with each other. The support going back and forth helped her to unlock code detail, to help her patients and the formulas she was transcribing (as input was needed for them).

All of this was done telepathically with tremendous laser focus. Once she was finished gathering the information needed, this dolphin would simply go out the tunnel and back to playing in the ocean. When this visual sequence finished I took in a breath as I released merging with this dolphins form. I was nudged in the side by this dolphin as if it was saying with a buddy slap of a fin "that was fun." As quickly as it began, this dolphin then reconnected with its pod and swam away. In that same exhale breathe a soft voice over me whispered "our session is complete."

I have been fascinated at how this entire cleanse has been blessed by spirit. During this month long journey there has been constant wonder and awe through gifts and experiences that are awaiting each of us within this work. I know that you too may be experiencing wonderful interludes from spirit aligning higher in your own development. We all get the joy of experiencing our own unique synchronicities in this month long journey. It is fun to discover (while thinking we are going to pursue one activity) only to have it unfold into so much more. Divine timing will just click, as we align in flow with enough time and resources to create our needed experiences. This healing was indeed my initiation into this final spiral of spirit.

Another positive addition to this day is the beginning of a lemon balm tincture to help increase joy in this phase. My herbalist made a special tincture for me to help increase joy while walking both worlds. I know for me personally sometimes the spirit world feels so good that coming back to reality can be too dense or abrupt at times. Lemon balm can balance and harmonize the emotional shifts between these two realms, to minimize the gap between them and stabilize our emotional energy more.

Day twenty one affirmations:

I am initiated into the next level on my spiritual path

I am open to an increased flow from spirit

I release anything that is keeping me from full vision

I forgive and release any patterns limiting my spirit

I easily harmonize the spirit plane with the earth plane

Day twenty one meditation and prep:

1. What am I guided to do for an initiation ceremony? (walking a self made labyrinth, working with a competent high integrity healer, most forms of bodywork ask to be led to your highest experience)

2. What do I know I need to improve upon to be with and in spirit more often? (early morning and late night meditation, setting up personal prayer alter, inside or outside home sacred space)

3. How can I prioritize my personal time to communicate more with spirit? (up earlier or later

alone to pray/meditate, communicating this need of respecting sacred time to your family, time alone to connect in nature)

4. What can I eat or do to assist this process today? (fasting for some, juicing or a raw day for others, follow what works for you)

5. What can I wear, or accent within the indigo blue shades to help assist this process? (amethyst, flowers, clothing and accessories in the indigo cobalt blue range)

Day twenty two

Day twenty two: throat center – (5th chakra) – sky blue – inbound spirit spiral - **Active expression (or silence) to experience and share highest truth from your throat chakra.**

As we enter the throat center, we can voice new priorities and clarify our spiritual goals. The deep sky blue at the base of the throat will have two separate days within this spiral of spirit, which are today and day 29. Today's focus is about organizing energy within this center to achieve a harmony that allows our highest creative expression here. So for today the priority is to simply observe and reevaluate past fifth chakra day notes to find where you may be over editing your truth or withholding in any way from your own full expression. Stay open to releasing lower integrity issues keeping you out of higher frequency and flow here.

We all have loved ones, family and friends who want us to fit into their snapshots or images of us. We all hold pictures of each other and need to constantly redefine and update these films as we all grow and evolve. Your increasing awareness and personal unfoldment may bring you to a fork in the road in many relationships. Should you find yourself here, know that this is only an opportunity to redefine your boundaries. Upgrading this can give yourself and others new and better parameters to live in. Staying open in this process should improve your relationships that are worth keeping.

For others who do not approve of your growth, or wish to control you, this process can be a nightmare. Should this happen, it is important to voice what your needs are, then to redefine yourself into a healthier territory. Surrender the entire relationship to the universe to either heal or release it, so you can both be free.

As we strive for constant expansion in our life, we may find many relationships will shift, creating new dynamics for us all. The blessing of this is that through detachment, non-judgment, and acceptance we all keep free from ceilings, and can thrive in our highest potential. The challenge of this is learning to live with constant shifts. Then we must be able to let go within these shifts, to the point of not really being defined at all in life.

Here we begin to live free, and are moved as simple spirit in action fulfilling the purpose and divine mission we are each specifically here to complete. The spirit spiral is indeed unique because this is not a physical cycle of reaching. Nor is it a mental cycle of visualization, leading one to an outward action. This spiral is a cycle of spirit, which is about receiving and allowing in the resonance of divine essence within every breath, to then continually flow with this higher frequency.

pm journal: Day grew more quiet as it wore on. Had a relaxing evening while ear candling. It was nice to clear out the sinuses, to open the fifth center more. I felt a deep processing all day from shifts that occurred yesterday. Silence is often the only way to let the filament stirred up in our pond (which is normal in doing any emotional work), to all settle back down.

Remember this is a cycle and spiral of allowing. So if this spiral feels different here than the others, just keep the faith while remaining still. Surrender and let spirit shift you for the better.

Day twenty two affirmations:
I release any editing of my personal truth in life
I now only share my fullest expression of self
I listen within and hear my direction from spirit with ease
I release anything keeping me out of creative truth
I allow my highest reality and live it today

Day twenty two mediation prep:

1. What relationships or environments do I need to redefine today? (speaking your truth where it is needed, engaging everything with purpose)

2. What needs to be complete so I can live in full expression for the rest of my life? (New commitment or contract with spirit to honor from now on)

3. What can I heal and reorganize in this area today? (ear candling, facial, shoulder massage, yoga to open this area with camel pose, fish pose, plow pose, toning)

4. Where if anywhere do I need to go (or do) to

start a new slate of self commitment to change here? (ocean, or any nature spot to inspire new contract with spirit, therapy, body work)

5. What can I wear, or accent with to assist this process today? (blue topaz, larimar, sapphire to bright sky blue, ginger, thyme, blue malva tea,)

Day twenty three

Day twenty three: heart center – (4th chakra) – green – inbound spirit spiral - **Surrendering any outstanding unforgiveness or heartache to spirit for healing**.

Today is one of two heart chakra days within this spiral to complete all unfinished forgiveness or grieving issues with the help of spirit. The next and final heart center day will end where we began in the core source point, (or God center). Today the focus is on what we can do to increase our connection from the lower to the higher chakras. With our whole system balanced, it is easy to clear any miscommunication within the physical and or emotional bodies.

am journal: Slept beautifully last night. Starting to fall asleep immediately, which I have not done in a long time. My head feels great this morning from the ear candling last night. Today is bright but still very cold outside on this emerald morning. I can feel a deep breakthrough has happened, although it is still in process and not fully on the surface just yet, where I can make linear sense of it. Made several changes to my prayer alter this morning.

I am really looking forward to a solid final week of cleansing, and keep praying for assistance to stay disciplined. This morning I am drinking a lemon green tea with cayenne pepper and fresh squeezed lemon to help circulate more, and to help stimulate the liver. Today is also a great day to reach out and share in whatever way you are guided to. If you stay open, an opportunity will present itself for you to extend out to another. It may be a charitable letter in your mail asking for a donation (to a cause that rings true for you). Or someone you come across who needs help, which provides you the gift of an opportunity to share from the joy of an open heart (not out of the mind through imposed mental obligation). Feel your contributions and give them consciously.

A healthy heart is the result of balanced give and take in life. We can see this literally in balanced blood flow to and from the heart organ in a physically healthy system. The same principle also happens spiritually by our sharing heartfelt wisdom, then equally receiving our own nourishing heart light from the universe. Not a bleeding heart healer that gives every ounce, only to wither in the corner due to lack of self care. Share fully by all means, but temper that with receiving the nourishment, breath and blood you need to fill your own chambers first. Only then can we re-emerge into the world to share again.

Accomplishing this balance in every chakra is our objective to attain by the end of this thirty day period. To release then redefine the mind and boundaries needed to accelerate our own path on every plane. Then to flow forward with spirit into our light work no matter what form our path shows up as. When we know who we are and can live in full power of our truth, we can then give and receive in whole capacity. Maintaining this high frequency flow is truly living an illuminated life.

Day twenty three affirmations:

My heart center is completely clear and balanced

Today I forgive and completely release the past

I give myself permission to open my heart fully

I open and feel new consciousness spinning within

I complete anything keeping me out of divine intimacy

Day twenty three meditation and prep:

1. What forgiveness issues or people are still outstanding in this center? (family, friends, co-workers, self-release, etc)

2. Who can I free today through forgiveness (so that I am free to)? (who comes to mind first? –start there)

3. Where can I go to get into a safe space to allow healing in this chakra? (nature, get away space, caring friends, alternative spa away)

4. What can I do to act on self-love for myself, as well as sharing this with others today? (a bubble bath, lovingly cooked homemade soup is very healing, then share as guided)

5. What can I eat, wear or accent with to assist this process today? (all emerald green items, spinach, wheatgrass, celery, stones: malachite, chysocolla, Gaia stone, emerald, peridot, green tourmaline.

Day twenty four

Day twenty four: solar plexus center – (3rd chakra) – yellow – inbound spirit spiral - **Reprogramming our power center into more balance for ongoing right use of personal power.**

Today is our final day in the third chakra, and a wonderful opportunity to align our power with that of spirit. When we are guided to our divine path, at some point we may see that our path is but a creek aligning into a great river. This river flows into yet a larger ocean of purpose, connected to the global wave. What we become within this wave of spirit is so much bigger than any ego quest. Here lies the true divine flow. In other words the ego wants to be its own puddle in control and predictably stagnate. Spirit naturally aligns us to every cell in the ocean flowing around the planet. Our single drop in this wave continues on absorbing into the atmosphere to merge with the infinite cosmos. We always have free will and get to choose whether we participate as the unconscious puddle, or as conscious active infinite space.

As we follow through, heal, and divine everything around us within this flow, we may realize we are simply conductors of this lightning. We do our part where it is called for, and then move on. There is nothing to fear or feel inferior about. If we think we are carrying the world on our shoulders, then we should be terrified. When we have surrendered and trust assistance with all things, there is no fear. When we finally attain consistent inner peace, we can rest in the knowing that we have indeed gotten out of our own way.

The level of any fear present in life will equal the level we are not surrendering to spirit. I know this is easier said than done. When I lived in Denver eons ago, I used to walk down a dark alley around three am to get home from work. Yet when I prayed for guidance on where to park, and walk, I could let go and trust that I was safe. Some nights while I was walking under fresh police crime tape (entering the alley to my apartment) this took tremendous faith to trust that spirit would guide me home safely.

am journal: Woke up with old low esteem patterns circling me. "What do you think you are doing? Why do you think anyone is going to benefit from this work?" I prayed for help to stop this inner upset. I listened to the part of me that was obviously out of its comfort zone today. My ego and power chakra were kicking up an inner critic about whether this was safe to work on, while whining in low esteem.

At any time during this cleanse should you find a chakra to be low or weak, congratulate yourself for being half way through the process of changing it. Finding and then naming weakness and vulnerability is part of the process towards healing it. Learning the subtle fluctuations in our patterns and natural rhythm is crucial in our soul development. When we support our own system with the frequency of color and light that it needs, this allows our weaknesses to surface in order to be honored (not judged), and then lovingly shown a new better method.

Today I mixed bright canary yellow, while carrying yellow and purple gemstones together. The combination of these two colors calls personal power into a higher state of purpose. Sadly most people in the world today seek power to dominate over situations and other people. Our misunderstanding and abuse of power in general gives this area and even the word 'power' a bad reputation, instead of the significant attention it deserves.

Without a strong sense of self or knowing how to express your own power, we can often exhaust ourselves in reaction to others. Or worse attach to everyone in ongoing power struggles that keep us constantly in our own way. Right use of power flows from a mutual cooperation with everyone. We all have something incredible to offer the world by doing our part, regardless of whether it sells, or is ever even seen. Trust this truth while in your own process of creating anything. It does not matter whether your divine assignment is a literal child, book, company, or project of any shape that needs inner confidence and strength of spirit to power it through to completion.

Day twenty four affirmations:
I balance and experience my divine power today
I forgive negative self talk keeping me
out of healthy power
I am a divine being embracing my wholeness today
Everything around me supports my power
Everyone around me shares a fair power exchange

Day twenty four meditation and prep:

1. Where is my level of power/self confidence rate from a number 1-6? (1-2 low 3-5 ideal 6+ too agressive for balance here – just ask)

2. What can I do today to balance my sense of self and personal power? (release draining friends or relationships, honoring time to nurture and build self and inner strength as guided, release unhealthy competition)

3. What can I do today to build my sense of self and power? (sunshine, lifting weights, rock climbing, self-care, sitting by fire, fresh sunlight)

4. What boundaries can I improve to keep my energy high? (letting others be, instead of exchanging negative commentary, removing all outside drains from your life)

5. What can I wear, eat, or accent with to support this process? (bright happy yellow, sunflowers, citrine, tangerine essence, grapefruit, lemon, banana, yellow topaz, think playfully, engage in exuberant kindness)

Day twenty five

Day twenty five: sacral center – (2nd chakra) – orange – inbound spirit spiral – **Upgrading your personal boundaries for greater spiritual harmony**.

Today we awaken the final sacral chakra day while entering the core of the spirit spiral. You think I would be done questioning spirit at this point, but again at first glance this did not make logical sense to me (that the sacral would be at the core) of the spirit phase? Then I remembered that we must be able to assimilate information that comes in through spirit in a way that we can absorb, understand, and then utilize here on the earth plane.

If we are not fully present and capable to do this on all levels (physically, emotionally and spiritually) then all the upward reaching will not manifest properly here. We must be able to apply these visions to create our world service. This is achieved by processing and then birthing higher insights here on the earth plane. Manifesting higher quality forms such as new technologies to preserve our planets resources, or whatever your sacred mission is here.

When our sacral center is running efficiently, we can incorporate high voltage insights into our everyday life. Doing this helps to raise the consciousness around us by just being able to hold our own boundary line while also interpreting our surroundings. When we use a strong sacral center in a practical manner it can help others alongside us on our path from our own healthy example. Therefore the sacral orange is a very relevant color for the core of spirit.

Next we will leave the through the base chakra with full grounding to stabilize our upgraded connection to spirit. My Indian Reiki and Magnified healing teacher Renuka Kumar shared her tremendous wisdom with me. She used to remind me: "If you are not fully grounded and present here on earth, then all of the astral work and travel is useless." She used to tease me that although I could reach so far up and out, what I really needed was more grounding to be here as a human being. I knew we had divinely crossed paths to work together, because she herself holds such a beautiful calm grounded space naturally at her healing center, Core Radiance.

am journal: Crazy dreams last night. Saw myself with several other women, all in beautiful greatly detailed ancient ceremonial gowns. There was a large stone table with a huge spread of gorgeous fresh flowers and tropical orchids set out next to us, that we were all admiring before this special event began. A tall man also dressed up (who everyone seemed quite fearful of) put the only lei of all white orchids around my neck. The rest of the women were given single flowers, although I was not sure of the significance of this. I was grateful to be 'chosen,' only to look up and see disapproving scowls darting from everyone around me. I then noticed the woman standing next to me had incredibly large, green emerald rings on each of her fingers. I looked down at my own right hand and had two of these incredible huge green rings on the second and fourth finger, then two purple rings on the third and fifth fingers. I gazed at their beauty and wondered where they came from. I knew we were all vying for the affections of this leader. Although you think this would be a joyful setting, I was actually trying to figure out an escape from this place all together.

pm journal: Had large fresh carrot juice today and raw cacao cookie with orange essence that was delicious. PM yoga to mellow down in the evening, also feeling beautifully centered and sensuous after this blessing of a day.

Day twenty five affirmations:

I take what I need in life and easily release the rest
I absorb everything easily and get the input I need
I assimilate my spiritual insights with ease
I release anything that is blocking my progress here
I now strengthen my digestive stamina

Day twenty-five meditation prep:

1. What can I do to balance this area today? (evaluate your spiritual strength to take in and use insights, then release what is not of high integrity)

2. How can I strengthen this area for spirit? (simplify, simplify, simplify, decide not to be distracted by people and projects keeping you off path)

3. What can I do to support this process? (journaling to connect the dots to find what is working for you, releasing what is not)

4. What diet would best serve this area for ongoing balance? (enzyme support, probiotics crucial in the gut here, liquid trace minerals, seaweed, high quality blue green algae creates the building blocks to rebuild cellular integrity here, also orange foods such as peaches, apricots, butternut squash, citrus, and so on)

5. What can I wear or accent with to support this center today? (bright happy tangerine orange, all orange flowers such as marigolds, orchid varieties, gemstones such as citrine, carnelian, orange calcite, or orange tone accents you come across are wonderful to remind you to increase your vitality here)

Day twenty six

Day twenty six: base center – (1st chakra) – red – outbound spirit spiral - **Grounding base chakra spiritual energy to manifest fully from spirit to the earth plane**.

Today represents the initial unwinding from the core. Being the final base center day this represents leaving ones spiritual core, to reemerge into the world as a clarified spiritually integrated being. This grounding actually comes from the core of our planet up into the soles of the feet, knees, and into the base center at the bottom of the spine to ground and nurture us fully. The base red is symbolic of new blood coursing through every cell to circulate throughout our entire system today, as we celebrate our upgraded wholeness.

These final few days on the outward ring are an affirmation to the world around us declaring our new contract to spirit. This first outbound ring symbolizes our commitment to honor and live from this higher level from now on. Today is a day of rebirthing into higher integrity and connection with all things. Now we can honor life around us more, and celebrate freedom through complete forgiveness. Here the past no longer holds any power over us. We are now free to commune with the divine in every breath.

am journal: Up late from sleeping so deep. Yesterdays acupuncture appointment worked on sacral center. I also kept hearing "adjust blood points" which I told my acupuncturist. She agreed that there were indeed several points to help strengthen the blood. This past weekend I went through an herbal book and knew that my body needed red clover and dong quai, which are both great female and blood nourishing herbs. I knew these two herbs would be very beneficial for me to follow up with after this month to help rebuild my system, once this clearing out phase is complete.

The common denominator in all of these herbs was the blood nourishing properties to help transfuse my system with an upgraded nutrient rich blood. Especially after all of this effort cleansing, it does not make sense for any of us to go back to old habits to just build up toxicity in the system again. Now the route of regeneration and high quality nutrition is the way to maintaining this higher frequency of health.

I have to admit the hardest part of this month for me has been to release my espresso in the morning. I have had some mornings without it, and have been alright. Other mornings especially without sleep, I have succumbed to organic coffee. Although this change for me here is a process, I do feel stronger each day without it. I could tell that caffeine was losing its grip when I would make it through the morning with enough energy then find my cup on the counter later in the afternoon still more than half full of coffee I did not finish. It is better to go slow with a change instead of forcing it (only to fall back into pattern from frustration) because the change was too drastic. Chicory coffee as many of you may know, is a roasted herbal natural coffee made from grains, fruits, and chicory root which is great when you like a robust flavor in the morning (without the caffeine).

I also use mate teas that are loose leaf, and find them a close second to chicory coffee. Both of these are wonderful for the body because they are adding minerals, and enhancing digestion. Instead of depleting minerals and increasing acidity like regular coffee can (actually taking from the body instead of giving). By my not giving up (or hiding my own truth about loving coffee here), I hope that you stay the course through your own diet goals as well. It can take time to create lasting core change, especially with strong addictives like caffeine or alcohol.

Dressed in coffee brown (no obsession intended), with a red fleece vest this morning. Then I picked out a small garnet, bloodstone, and red coral, to help support this base center today energetically. There have been insights for the last few days in my meditation work about reprogramming my blood for greater immunity strength. Our blood and bones are incredible the way they reflect our strength. While also holding ancient knowledge and cellular patterns from centuries ago. If you have ever confirmed anything in your life because "you know it in your bones," this is exactly what it means. I believe when we connect fully with spirit, and get our lives on purpose all of the time, our system upgrades and sensitizes to things around us whether we want it to or not.

When I began to avidly pursue a more spiritual life, my own personal overhaul began that to this day evaluates several dimensions simultaneously. When we begin to live in this high zone without bringing our bodies and minds up in balance alongside this spiritual awakening, this can cause an overall imbalance. It also keeps one too focused on maintenance of either physical challenges, or mental distractions. We may wonder about ever hitting our stride, which sometimes stems from the constant reactive stress of scattered energy that is usually just one of our imbalanced spirals being used inefficiently.

As we expand and continually open our mind to higher awareness, we will continually see additional layered dimensions to everything we encounter. Then should we choose to live dedicated to spirits lead, life becomes an ongoing miracle. This is not always easy or fun, but the rewards of a balanced life with spirit (once radically experienced) will not be exchanged for any other life. With that said, this final grounding day of red is our final day to root to Mother earth. You may wish to hold the intention to keep your grounding throughout the rest of your life. This is important so you can manifest your path here fully, to complete what you alone were born to do.

Day twenty six affirmations:
I am fully grounded and supported by the earth
It is safe for me to live my truth and path
I commit to keeping grounded while working with spirit
I walk in both worlds with grounding and clarity
I am perfectly rooted at the depth that is right for me

Day twenty six meditation prep:

1. What do I need to drain or release on this final out flowing day? (colonics, mud bath, outdoor natural springs, napping on the ground outside)

2. Where do I need to go to ground deeper today? (outside meditation, sit with your back to the trees, deeper in nature if possible)

3. What can I do to activate this earth element today? (sculpting with red clay, gardening, setting border rocks out around a garden)

4. What does my body want today to feed my blood? (vitex plant leaf iron, wheatgrass, dong quai, iron rich kale, dark greens, red foods like beets, prunes, all high in iron)

5. What can I accent with to support this process today? (red items, garnet, bloodstone, red coral,

flowers, chili peppers, cranberries, all red flowers roses, orchids)

Day twenty seven

Day twenty seven: crown center – (7th chakra) – violet – outbound spirit spiral - **Achieving greater personal vision of soul path within the crown chakra**.

Today is a day of incoming vision. Try to include as much silence or meditation space as possible. For all mothers reading out there, I know this can be a challenge with small children. I currently home school myself, and have two young elementary students bantering and debating in the background as I write here. So I know the discipline required to keep focused. Yet these challenges, distractions, and to do lists are not going to disappear. Our job is to rise to them and increase our own life force in the process. We can do better than just surviving or "getting through it all." We are here to live our life passionately, not just get through it.

Instead of surviving we can dance through life enthusiastically, in constant joy, while holding our center and meeting our needs. Doing this well takes immense conscious focus and life force. Yet this is the practical crux of what this labyrinth offers. It is meant to simplify and clear out the items or diet aspects that are stealing your energy. Then you can gently replace lower energy habits with higher ones, so you can live more efficiently in every way.

Today alongside your work and daily schedule, exclude yourself to as much needless chit chat as possible, and just drink in the silence. Be outside as much as you can alone for time to call in your higher self. Stay open to receive your next step. Trust that you will hear it. Keep a journal close by to record patterns, symbols, or phrases that may not make sense right away. Over time (as you maintain high integrity intentions) this will make sense and create a direction that is right for you. Often times we are given a small piece of a bigger puzzle. Once it is all together, the whole picture can be really miraculous to witness. It is healing for us to get confirmation and then realize that we did hear spirit correctly from that first small puzzle piece. This will also build trust in your relationship with the universe, so you can handle more input as you are ready for it.

Today is a day of music, swirling like a dervish, cat naps in the sun, and as for me I'll be climbing trees.

I have been a tree panther since I was young, always having a barefoot connection while high in a mighty oak or banyan overlooking the Floridian jungle below. Whatever brings you that same sense of childlike wonder is what you need to find and follow today.

Perhaps it is finding extra time to sleep, in order to allow a visionary dream to appear. Please record your dreams, especially in these final days. Even violent or strange dreams should have significant meaning. They are often just release work, showing us fears we are overcoming. Or prophetic insight into your future may be revealed. No matter what you magnetize in these final days simply remain open and receptive to receive the messages your dreams may bring you.

am journal: Up 5am. Last night I realized that I have opened and shifted in a way that had really pushed me out of my comfort zone in my marriage. I realized through meditation that the visual of my marriage was now stuck and tight. It needed to lighten and stretch this out if we were going to grow and stay healthy. As our circle extends out we must upgrade (our end) of the relationships around us to keep our frequency harmonious with those we love. No drama here, just redefining fresh boundaries and space where it is needed.

I sat outside in my meditation corner to do some

light sculpting on this contorted image of my relationship. I watched this symbolic shape twist and expand as the color shifted from a dark and tightly woven orb to a stretched out violet pink translucent sphere with an increased space in between the lines. After a few minutes of light work the stretching of this visual holographic image shifted in both color and sound. I watched old layers spin out and away from this orb. Doing this light work (or I like to call light sculpting) helped me to breath deeper and forgive where I was holding onto old patterns within myself in the outer fields.

On an energetic level this was also releasing old dynamics from our relationship that were now outmoded. Doing this opened me to receive new breathing room and better reflections to potentially heal us both. After this release and prayer were complete this concern transformed into a genuine deep peace.

If you feel major inner shifts today, trust that they are moving you in a higher direction. Getting used to the unknown and sometimes chaotic pattern of the infinite possibility does take stamina, and constant faith. We must build and live this strength more each day in order to climb to our own highest peak.

Day twenty seven affirmations:

I am open to a higher vision for my life

I am fully receptive to the highest healing light of spirit

I feel and record my incoming shifts today

My circle of experience now expands forever

I embrace a higher way of being in my life

Day twenty seven meditation prep:

1. What can I do to upgrade my energetic standards today? (evaluate your environment, relationships, ask for direction here)

2. Where can I go to connect to my divine source? (nature, local park, quiet time daily is now crucial)

3. How can I strengthen my connection to my guides more? (toning, soft instrumental music, natural water source (or nature music)

4. What diet is appropriate today? (eating light, juicing, master cleanse, or fasting if appropriate for you)

5. What can I accent with to support this center today? (white, lavender tones, stones: spirit quartz, amethyst, purple fluorite, lotus tea, lots of water today)

*special gemstone/crystal note: this is a great time to clear your crystals by leaving them out in the sun or moonlight for a day or two. I am going to clear my collection for three days outside to allow them all to attune higher.

Chapter Ten

Completing the Circle

Day twenty eight

Day twenty eight: third eye center – (6th chakra) – cobalt blue – outbound spirit spiral – **Attuning your third eye to a higher vision of soul path in your life**.

am journal: Incredible dream. I was driving really fast with a man sitting in the front passenger seat next to me, while aware of two other women in the backseat. Then the man next to me pointed out the window to a rainbow starlight diamond like prism following us over the car that was to the right of us in the sky. This small rainbow colored light looked like a diamond ring sun reflection with its brilliance in color, with all of the sparkling rainbow tones shimmering within it.

I looked up into this light and was immediately transfixed by an internal magnetic force drawing me into this radiance. Although the car kept speeding along the road at an incredible pace, I became fixated and awe inspired by this now expanding light and tremendous magnetic force pulling me up from the sky. Then the colors began to shift into a translucent pastel colored mist until the ascended master Christ appeared so huge that he was taller than the clouds. He did not saying anything, but smiled as he held my awe inspired gaze. He held out the familiar image of the swirling heart with a flame in it. I could not move from this magnetic force and felt the expansion happening within me from seeing Christ getting stronger with each moment. I even closed my eyes for a second turning away. Yet when I re-opened my eyes, he was still there just as before, smiling. The sensation of looking at this intense radiance was almost more than I could handle physically or emotionally. After what felt like a few minutes this image shifted again into a pinkish cloud and dissolved back into the clear blue sky.

The next thing I knew I was walking along on Pearl Street in downtown Boulder, Colorado where I used to live. I was on a private tour with a woman who was preparing to open a large Tibetan style alternative healing and yoga center. The holistic center was in a high end gorgeous immense sacred space with many colorful rooms. One room was a deep lotus fuchsia, while another was a rich royal blue. Each room shifted in dramatic color with a different motif and animal statue, or picture, all reflecting India's beauty and inspiration throughout the center.

She had many large, authentic statues including Ganesh, Buddha and Kuan Yin, all collected from her own travels to India and beyond. The back of the center had a large meeting room with comfortable round pillows on the floor and even high chairs if guests wanted to enjoy some tea during lectures there. They served lotus seed and other specialty teas, and even had small vegan snacks for events and sacred gatherings. Some rooms were smaller than others, but most were still empty (since this center was still being put together) and not open to the public just yet. Each room also had a unique wall piece of individual design. Some had complex mandalas or symbols, while others had beautiful artwork, or statues of animals. One teal blue room had a large white elephant, while another room was a rich coral with a Siberian tiger painting on the wall, but again no furniture was moved in just yet.

Once the tour was complete we were standing outside on the street corner as she showed me flyers, plans and programs she was preparing (that were meant to be added in later). I nodded in excitement for her, feeling honored that she respected my opinion enough for me to help add input, and even the chance to tour this sacred healing space.

Next thing I knew I was at a gathering in this same healing center, working with many women, all from different cultures. We were thrilled to be together, sharing an incredible resonance as a group. We were all laughing and joyfully preparing for the grand opening like children preparing for a holiday. We began to make gift pieces for many famous speakers coming in, and prepared pumpkin soup in coconut hulls for the opening party.

When I looked down to see what I was wrapping, it was a small white silk purse (like you would find in China town). Inside was a small silver piece with the ascended master Christ's face on it. I was again transfixed and felt attuned by seeing his face. I glanced around at others in the group who were happily wrapping everything from little Buddha's, to ancient symbols. One of the women working in the center asked if I had received her phone message. She shared that they wanted me to teach yoga classes, and be part of the opening healing team. My heart sank when I shared that I was a healing practitioner, and although I practiced yoga, I was not formally trained to teach it. "I know they really want you to teach here" she continued, "and they have a schedule ready for you." I was confused by this and asked to speak to the owner. "You should talk to her about what you want to do, because they are ready to hire you," she continued with sincerity. Then my eyes fluttered open and I was spinning in awe of this intensely vivid dream. I also found it wild to have such a powerful dream (when all of my crystals were out in my garden through the night) to clear.

Being a student of the Course in Miracles has definitely deepened my relationship to the ascended master Christ. Not in any religious sense, but in the true essence of following his teachings as an ascended master to help each of us to live an enlightened existence here, to unite the world in light. Honestly, I am not entirely sure what either of these dreams I've had the last few nights are supposed to mean. All I know is that I do feel powerfully changed by them (even physically). I have a sense that life will reveal markers over time, to confirm and reveal their significance. Trust your own dreams at this time as well.

Our job is to do our part and stay diligent to the signs that cross our path along the way. This entire month has supplied us all with ongoing stepping stones for us to explore and heal from, as we put one foot in front of the other. For me this came through books, people, and animals along the way. The universe simply pours blessing forth through wisdom, abundance, and knowledge that I share here through my own experience. Trust what the universe puts in your path as well.

pm journal: Brilliant walk on the beach today. After time admiring the shoreline, I then created another large simple labyrinth in the sand. I used azurite and sodalite in my labyrinth. Going into the spiral, I affirmed my intention to more fully open my talents and spiritual gifts to be able to fully activate my divine mission here. I stopped at the core and prayed with immense gratitude for all of the angelic, goddess, ascended masters, and universal support from so many light filled beings that help me in every step.

Then while slowly circling outward I stopped at the end of the spiral sensing a beautiful wave of closure. Something was complete within me after going through this introspective period. This phase was closing, and I could now sense a deep level of inner completion. I also knew the next phase for me was to now turn outward, and begin to assist others through this same journey. I also understood clearly how many health challenges I had endured from birth, and through my childhood, had divinely educated and prepared me to guide others at such a high level now.

Day twenty eight affirmations:

I pay attention to dreams and visions coming in today

I align fully to spirits lead for my path from now on

I see and know my place in the world

I trust the direction that I am being led

I am always in the right place within divine timing

Day twenty eight meditation prep:

1. Have I seen or heard anything from spirit that I need to contemplate? (recheck your dream journal, mediation insights, or whispers that may be constant regarding change)

2. Where can I get away to allow time to receive from spirit today? (nature, time alone even in a sea salt bath, meditation, labyrinth walk)

3. How can I activate this area more and open this center? (Aryuvedic shirodhara hot oil ajna treatment, castor oil rubbed in a circle on the third eye, yoga, pranayama breathing, and poses to open, chanting Om)

4. What can I supplement to support this area? (Harmonic Innerprizes Etherium Gold, Pink, Aulterra, or any Bach tincture you feel guided to)

5. What can I wear or accent with to assist this process? (Cobalt or indigo blue items, lapis lazuli, dark

red grapes, blueberries, hibiscus flower tea)

Day twenty nine

Day twenty nine: throat center – (5th chakra) – sky blue – outbound spirit spiral - **Expressing your upgraded standard of personal truth to the world**.

Speak up today to outwardly express your higher truth and path fearlessly. Today is a day of divine expression as we emerge into the outer ring of this spiral. It is an opportunity to sing out and voice our truth without hesitation, as we feel drawn to do so. However this power is not to be used to knock down every critic's door to prove anything (which would only deplete our newfound strength). Instead speak up when appropriate, in situations that are opportunities for you to share your expanded light with others. Use your light in a way that will energize and enlighten everyone.

am journal: Went to the beach this morning wearing bright turquoise blue, with an Australian turquoise necklace. While walking along the shoreline, going through my daily balancing routine I felt a wonderful deep calm. I was guided as always through the right process for me in the moment, and simply followed along in visualization and prayer.

I was shown a beautiful multi colored macaw parrot that has been guiding me through this process. I laughed as I thought of a painting done earlier this year of several coconut palms with a small green parrot watching from the corner branch. This brilliant animal guide was to remind and inspire me to be bold, trust my own brilliance, and to stay illuminated. I began to notice people around me walking on the beach all had on bright neon orange, and pinky Key West colors. I nodded that "I got it" and would align to this increase in my energetic brightness now.

Every day on this cleanse has brought such immense blessings for me. I feel so lucky to be sharing it here with you in sincere hopes that it heals and expands your life and potential too. Although I was by no means perfect, if I look at the expectations I set on day one. I find the real success is not necessarily the diet score card, although this is an important aspect to develop. The true healing here is in the release of old self judgment, and any other mental or emotional blocks keeping us out of wholeness.

My old self-limiting patterns would have stopped cleansing within the first few days and then beaten myself up for a long time after, in both negative commentary, and further binging. If I was not strong enough to persevere with the help of spirit and strong will, you would not be reading this book right now. Learning to give yourself constant self love, patience and encouragement can heal your life beyond comprehension.

When I did slip up, I simply said "okay that moment is gone, let it go, forgive it, move forward and make better choices right now." I know this can be easier said than done, especially when we are under great stress. As we heal the emotional and mental undercurrents over time, we can release challenging substances. We can then learn to relish and savor wholeness instead. As we do our part where spirit leads, this expanded wholeness simply unfolds for us as we pursue change. One day we may realize that unconditionally loving ourselves and others is what frees us all to expand into oneness that we all deserve to live, love, and create from.

Day twenty nine affirmations:

I joyfully speak my truth

I voice my guided messages with love

I speak with compassion about everything

I acknowledge my creations with acceptance

I express my divinity through every word and action

Day twenty nine meditation prep:

1. What can I do to express my purpose today? (time in meditation clarifying path, energizing new creative work or play)

2. What (if anything) do I need to re-create or redefine in my life? (any last release or forgiveness issues to free up space to make room for the new)

3. Where can I go to assist or inspire new light in this center? (high altitudes, nature, outside celebrating sunrise or sunset, open spaces)

4. What small way will I express gratitude to the support around me? (thank the universe, clean up the beach or park, support environmental causes, thank friends and family for their support)

5. What can I wear, eat, or accent with today to support this center? (robin's egg or deep sky blue, turquoise, blue lace agate, blue malva tea)

Day thirty

Day thirty: inner and outer heart – (4th chakra) – pink and green together – fully circling the entire triple spiral back into the center point – **Illumination within the inner and outer heart chakra creating a greater activation of your trinity light within**.

Today we are re-emerging into the world with unconditional love, acceptance, and awakening. Wow you made it! We made it! Congratulations for making it to the end of this sacred journey. Day 30 is truly is a momentous day. Align with the highest healing light of universal support that has been alongside you through this entire time.

I love the analogy that when we really stretch outside of our comfort circle, how we not only increase our radius out further, but that we are also never return to the original smaller shape ever again. There is no going back, once you truly align and expand with spirit. It is everyone's job to unite and hold a higher light and standard for the world now. When we collectively hold a vision of the atmosphere regenerating, and all of the planets resources being respected, miracles will become visible.

am journal: What a beautiful day. I woke up in

the middle of the night to a mesmerizing rainstorm. I thought of my crystal collection still out in the garden. This morning's rich thunder, then rain, and now gentle sunshine has been a full circle in itself. Even the flow of this storm was a microcosmic reflection of this entire spiral cycle. We confronted our physical self in the north spiral to clear the body (breaking the dense physical through thunder). We then moved through the mind to the east to release lower thought forms and defeating blocks from our inner visuals (melting away old patterns through the rain). To now complete this alignment, by allowing perfect sunlight to ignite higher self intelligence within (by merging with the sun) in our own personal core or center point.

For my final prayer session I lit more candles than usual, and began a gratitude meditation. I know this has been an incredibly healing process for me personally. The times I began to question or compare myself to anyone around me, the support of the universe always piped up to remind me to quiet my mind and just put my next foot forward.

Today we venture back to our starting point in the heart, found at the center of the trinity. We can celebrate and embrace this accomplishment today. Once we can maintain our own balance, we can then turn our light outward to illuminate the world. This radiance also extends through our feet, bringing light to the path ahead. It is with heartfelt thanks and gratitude I extend to you now, for sharing this experience with me. Hopefully by now you can see at least a few of the dimensional shifts we all can experience, as we strengthen enough to live in heaven and on earth, to consciously walk with them together at the same time.

My prayer is that this strengthens and awakens your senses long after this month is complete. I hope that you continue on a healthier, wiser, and more connected path from now on. Know that this is possible as we maintain our progress by honoring our body and our devotional time. As we put forth an ongoing determined effort to expand, the universe will support us through infinite resources.

Following the signs and guideposts along the way are easy when you are clear and living as spirit in action. Commit to living clear and things will continually flow toward higher experience. Some people think life should not change or be challenging once this core balancing happens. On the contrary, everything will continually change, no matter what we choose. Change is eternal whether we cleanse ourselves or not. So we can either drag along in the mud, wallowing around our own little ego puddle. Or glide along comfortably with the stardust of the cosmos, with the breath of spirit guiding our flight through the multiverse.

Day thirty affirmations:

I expand and align into greater wholeness today
I circulate new joy and exuberance on my path
I celebrate my journey and make everyday count
I always live my light and truth

Day thirty meditation prep:

1. What will I do to celebrate today? (dancing, running around in the dark under the stars, sharing your journey where you are guided to)

2. What am I going to commit to, in order to maintain this balance? (continuing on this higher self standard by keeping high quality food, people, and environments a priority, living green)

3. How will I share and receive more, as I expand forward? (commit to balancing all you give to the world, by caring for yourself and nurturing your own needs equally)

4. What ritual can I create or participate in today to give this healing journey a sense of completion? (creating a final labyrinth in or outside to

symbolize your experience, gratitude ceremony or prayer to honor the elements and support around you)

5. What can I accent with today to support this final celebration? (emerald or spring green everything, eat your greens, wheatgrass, kale, sprouts, green tea, rose quartz, green plants indoors, all herbs rosemary, basil, thyme)

*** please note:** Know that you can repeat this Spiral process at any time you are ready to go deeper into your own personal process. I repeat this 30 day process a few times a year and have found it to be a different dynamic every time I return to this sacred journey.

Quick Reference Guide

Daily diet, accent, and inspirations to support each chakra center

Just find the chakra day you are in, at the beginning of each day. Then choose one, two or all items that feel healing and appropriate for you. Remember these are just suggestions. There are many items not listed that are just as nourishing. Use what you come across within the color range you are in, and trust what feels right for your own process.

Daily chakra smoothie ideas:

Using hemp, flax seed, (or hemp powder) is my recommended protein of choice for any smoothie. Flax and hemp both contain quality omega oils that can keep you comfortably full until lunch, and slow your sugar absorption to help balance appetite. Please use locally wild and certified organic whenever possible for all ingredients to all recipes.

Smoothie shortcut: buying different organic frozen fruits in a variety of colors (blueberries, peaches, raspberries, so you can easily create the daily chakra colors without fuss). I also find this to be a budget saver since frozen organic tends to be cheaper often times as well, yet fresh is always best if you can find it.

blushing goddess shake:

1 Banana, ½ cup organic raspberries (or any red fruit)
1 tspn raw virgin coconut oil, organic coconut water
1-2 tbspns organic hemp seeds, or powder
½ cup unsweetened pomegranate juice
½ cup fresh pineapple
liquid b-12 complex +few drops colloidal silver
fresh shredded ginger

Remember to bless your shake with gratitude and healing prayer before you enjoy.

Juicing shortcut: Tinkerbell's green tonic is a great tip I created when I did not have time daily to juice fresh greens, but still wanted a higher quality juice throughout the week. It is also a budget booster since juicing can get expensive (especially the way my kids can drink it). I find this to be a fantastic way to stretch my grocery dollar, while keeping a high quality alkaline juice for several days at a time. It lets you juice once or twice a week instead of everyday which most of us may not have time to do.

Tinkerbell's Secret Green Tonic:

- large one gallon glass jug of Organic apple juice

-1-2 lemons (depending on your sour taste preference)

-fresh ginger (size of thumb)

-half of fresh kale bunch (any variety)

-whole bunch fresh organic celery

-fresh bunch organic parsley

I find this to keep fresh for about four to five days. My kids love it and this is also a great alkaline tonic to keep minerals high, which will help to purify the whole body. **Important Note: carrots/beets will spoil the juice much quicker while increasing sugar content so stick with what you like here in the green tones to make it last longer.*

Support/ personal recommendations:

Custom blend chakra herbal tinctures, teas, remedies

After completing the 30 day Spiral herself, Master herbalist Linda Nash Stevenson was inspired into creating her own custom chakra blends to use her wisdom to support others in the Spiral experience.

Linda Nash Stevenson, A.P. Dipl. Ac. Board Certified Acupuncture Physician & Master Herbalist

lifeforceacupuncture@yahoo.com

Chanakara.com has a seven chakra assortment of teas to support the entire chakra system. A simple investment of one box instead of trying to purchase or find each individual herb for each center daily. There are also many other varieties of teas that contain great flowers and herbs so see what you like and are drawn to at your health food store.

Crystals / gemstones

There is an optional 10 pc gemstones set you can order from **livingthespiral.com** to accompany your cleanse. The stone set will match the chakras that are listed and explained as **therapy stones** in the chakra list at the end of the resource guide. You can order this by emailing a request on our website. The set can vary with availability to order the stones but may include one sunstone, amethyst, sodalite, blue lace agate, aventurine, rose quartz, citrine, carnelian, red jasper, and black tourmaline. If you have your own stones, or want to use different ones altogether, that works too. These are just a suggestion to help open and increase your awareness, as you work to open and balance the chakras. I added this set for those who do not have access to quality stones, or are not sure what to start with. These stone sets are cleared, activated through energy work and blessed for the user before being released for sale. You can meditate with these by placing them on the chakra centers as you meditate. You can bathe with them, carry them in your pocket, sleep with them under your pillow or bed, or keep them in body work sessions to support your energy. Or you can simply carry each one with you for the day, to work with each chakra energy, and stone individually.

Spinning Lotus salad dressing:

1 cup seeded and cubed organic fresh ripe papaya – (add a few seeds if you like the spice)

2 tblspn lemon juice (zest optional)

1-2 large garlic clove(s)

2 tblspn organic extra virgin olive or flax oil

fresh chopped herbs of preference – basil, parsley, oregano, thyme, lemongrass (one or all)

Celtic sea salt or Himalayan pink salt / pepper to taste

Small to medium skinned fresh ginger piece

1 tblspn organic raw agave syrup

Just blend for great small batch and store fresh in fridge for several days. Use for salad, as veggie dip, or sandwich spread. Most salad dressings have low quality oils, too much sugar and fat so using this throughout the month is ideal.

Thailand Rainbow Nectar (great for all chakras)

2 cups fresh or 14 oz can organic coconut milk

1½ cups organic veggie broth

1+ tblspn fresh minced ginger (to taste)

1-2 fresh diced clove(s) garlic

bunch fresh diced cilantro/basil/Italian parsley

1 tspn fresh or dried Lemongrass

1-2 tblspn real maple syrup (or raw agave/yacon)

cayenne and fresh chili peppers (at heat preference)

1 whole lime squeezed (zest optional)

½ tspn Celtic sea salt – or Braggs to taste (I use both)

½ cup chopped red onion

½ cup chopped celery

½ cup finely chopped butternut squash

1 tspn sesame or extra virgin olive oil

2-3 tblspn fresh finely shaved coconut flakes (optional)

(you can add colors you need, such as carrot or beet for chakra focus within the day you are working on)

first step: add oil to pan on medium heat to sauté onions, celery, any other veggie, garlic, until a little softer. After a few minutes add Braggs, salt, fine coconut flakes, maple syrup, and spices. Next add broth and coconut milk along with every other ingredient (lime, cayenne, ginger, etc) and simmer on low heat for about 20 minutes. Add ½ fresh cilantro before, and ½ when serving, and or fresh scallions.

Basmati or brown rice is a nice addition, if you want a heartier soup. *for spice freaks like me feel free to add more fun extras like rosemary, thyme, lavender, and so on. They make the end result more complex, and although not for everyone (which is why they are not in the above recipe) for some they make all the difference for a soul soothing herbal remedy. Enjoy.

Basic daily menu/ 30 day overview:

AM Breakfast: One option I have almost daily is a smoothie, using any fruit of choice to match the chakra day. Be sure to add protein such as hemp seed, flax, or almond butter to help slow sugar absorption and give you excellent quality omega oils. If you feel you need eggs, oatmeal or just a break from the smoothie routine that is fine. Just keep your choices low in salt, fat, and portion to help you to keep clear.

AM/PM Snacks: throughout the day: plenty of fresh local in season vegetables and organic fruit. Also dehydrated crackers, raw nuts like almonds, raw pumpkin seeds, or air popped (not microwaved) popcorn are high quality snacks that can keep you full during the day.

Lunch/Dinner: try to have fresh salad with lemon juice and olive oil (or the above spinning lotus salad dressing). Eat protein according to your needs. Again just keep meals low in fat, sugar and salt. Use an iodized sea salt, or Celtic sea salt sparingly to season.

Desserts: Low fat sorbets (try making your own if you have the equipment), find low sugar and fat alternatives in the health food store to keep you feeling satisfied. Even a sweetened organic herbal tea or decaf chai can feel like a treat at night. If you take magnesium or calcium at night with your tea this can really sooth, and calm your nerves naturally.

Coffee/Teas: There are fantastic alternatives to coffee including chicory coffee. There are also great cleansing teas at the health food store that you may feel drawn to trying as well. Also available are custom made herbal chakra blend teas by Master Herbalist/Acupuncturist Linda Nash Stevenson.

Water: Remember lots of high quality water (add lemon or apple cider vinegar in morning if you like) can help flush out impurities as you cleanse. Pray into every glass of water before you drink it. See Dr. Emoto's 'Hidden Messages from Water' book and you will understand through his remarkable visuals, that water is indeed sentient to our vibration and can mirror our intention and thoughts. Use plain stickers to make your own chakra intentions to help support you more.

Cleansing products

When it comes to purchasing products to cleanse that are right for you, it takes some consideration especially since we are all at different levels of health, budget and goals. Remember many herbs can conflict with medications so be sure to check with your doctor before starting any program or any new product, that it is right and safe for you to use. What is healing for one person, may be detrimental for another. My website has several links of products I have personally used and recommend. Simply adjusting your diet to release all forms of sugar and salt will begin a cleansing affect in a sense, (if your body is used to large amounts of lower quality items). Remember lots of water, sweating, rest and exercise as you proceed will help your body transition easier.

Learn how to intuitively guide your own patterns on when and how much you should eat. Our schedules often dictate eating at times that confuse our bodies and natural rhythm. As we begin to ask and honor our individual needs we will each be guided into our own best practice of diet, rest, exercise, and meditation.

Creating your own labyrinth

When you wish to use a **spiral labyrinth** personally during the cleanse I recommend working with a single spiral for each ten day period. This not only keeps it simple, but helps you to focus on one part of the trinity (single ten day mini spirals) at a time. Using a simple twine to duplicate the spiral in the back of the book will help you to recreate this symbol in as simple, or complex of a design as you like. If this is not convenient simply using the color spiral on the back pages with a q-tip will create a perfect finger labyrinth for you to even do anywhere. Your own self-made labyrinth can be equally successful to a life size one, when your intention is clear enough.

Play, laugh, and make this your greatest adventure ever. You can recreate this spiral with rocks in your garden (or plants), sand, dirt, or anything you wish. Even try sidewalk chalk outside in your driveway. The purpose of this image is to hold this visual as a focal point, while walking the thirty day path. Trust your internal shifts along the way. Allow your process and laugh as much as you can along the way. Keep focused on your intentions and feel your walk. May love and light pour infinite blessings on you on every step along your own personal quest.

30 day snapshot chart

daily glance chart for those on the go

(look at each morning for quick daily focus)

day 1: chakra: **4th inner heart**

color to eat/wear/use: **pink (all shades)**

focus: **body consciously connecting to inner heart and universal source light**

day 2: chakra: **7th crown**

color to eat/wear/use: **lavender**

focus: **aligning to increased spiritual support for your physical goals**

day 3: chakra: **6th third eye**

color to eat/wear/use: **indigo blue**

focus: **increasing intuitive clarity about what physical changes are right for you at this time**

day 4: chakra: **5th throat**

color to eat/wear/use: **sky blue**

focus: **expressing physical changes you are ready to make to others who will positively support your personal goals**

day 5: chakra: **4th heart**

color to eat/wear/use: **green**

focus: **sharing generously while receiving what you need for your own support**

day 6: chakra: **4th inner heart**

color to eat/wear/use: **pink**

focus: **consciously connecting deeper to allow needed shifts within your core or center point**

day 7: chakra: **3rd power center**

color to eat/wear/use: **yellow**

focus: **increasing physical strength to direct your energy more efficiently**

day 8: chakra: **2nd sacral**

color to eat/wear/use: **orange**

focus: **resetting physical boundaries where they are needed to better support your needs**

day 9: chakra: **1st base**

color to eat/wear/use: **red**

focus: **grounding and increasing your physical stability to maintain changes you have created**

day 10: chakra: **transition**

color to eat/wear/use: **brown – grey**

focus: **grounding deeper within the earth – remaining stable while moving into the mind – remineralizing your body**

day 11: chakra: **1st base**

color to eat/wear/use: **red**

focus: **healing prosperity and personal safety issues to clear negative beliefs from the mind**

day 12: chakra: **2nd sacral**

color to eat/wear/use: **orange**

focus: **releasing and recycling old ideas and beliefs that no longer serve you - freeing up mental energy wasted on ego focus**

day 13: chakra: **3rd power**

color to eat/wear/use: **yellow**

focus: **clearing home of old energies for greater stamina and mental clarity**

day 14: chakra: **4th heart**

color to eat/wear/use: **green**

focus: **labyrinth walk to heal heart wounds or past grief that may still be haunting the mind**

day 15: chakra: **5th throat**

color to eat/wear/use: **sky blue**

focus: **expressing (or listening) to what you need to clarify about your goals and life path**

day 16: chakra: **6th third eye**

color to eat/wear/use: **indigo blue**

focus: **clearing old records updating personal information for greater peace of mind**

day 17: chakra: **7th crown**

color to eat/wear/use: **lavender**

focus: **integrating parts of the mind that are scattered – clarifying personal direction**

day 18: chakra: **8th astral gold**

color to eat/wear/use: **gold/silver**

focus: **aligning to healing sun essence from the astral level to illuminate the mind**

day 19: chakra: **7th crown**

color to eat/wear/use: **lavender**

focus: **integrating higher light into the whole system from a greater divine connection**

day 20: chakra: **transition**

color to eat/wear/use: **brown - grey**

focus: **grounding light while reconnecting to the earth so we can practically use this new energy**

day 21: chakra: **6th third eye**

color to eat/wear/use: **indigo blue**

focus: **clearing all senses for greater spiritual attunement**

day 22: chakra: **5th throat**

color to eat/wear/use: **sky blue**

focus: **active expression (or silent contemplation) about sharing oneself in greater spiritual truth**

day 23: chakra: **4th heart**

color to eat/wear/use: **green**

focus: **surrendering any outstanding forgiveness issues to spirit**

day 24: chakra: **3rd power**

color to eat/wear/use: **yellow**

focus: **reprogramming ones personal power for right use with spirits direction**

day 25: chakra: **2nd sacral**

color to eat/wear/use: **orange**

focus: **aligning with spirit for appropriate boundaries to better support your soul path**

day 26: chakra: **1st base**

color to eat/wear/use: **red**

focus: **grounding spiritual energy to manifest fully here on the earth plane**

day 27: chakra: 7th **crown**

color to eat/wear/use: **lavender**

focus: **higher alignment for greater personal vision of soul path**

day 28: chakra: **6th third eye**

color to eat/wear/use: **indigo blue**

focus: **allowing greater sight and knowing of soul work - releasing ego pursuits and related illusions keeping you off your higher path**

day 29: chakra: **5th throat**

color to eat/wear/use: **sky blue**

focus: **speaking higher personal vision in truth from whole spirit**

day 30: chakra: **4th inner heart**

color to eat/wear/use: **pink/green**

focus: **activation of trinity light within self to reach your highest soul path**

*See **chakra chart** to follow on next page
for greater daily support and resources and in depth information to clear each individual chakra.

Golden sun/starlight chakra (8th)

Colors to wear/accent with: gold, silver, white

Location of chakra: arms length above head at fingertips

Element: sunlight/starlight essence

Energetic ability: divine essence of Christ consciousness

Protein: hemp seed or powder, raw almonds

Juice: coconut milk or juice, fresh pineapple

Fruit/Veg: papaya, mango, coconut, golden beet, daikon radish

Herbs: wintergreen or mint, vanilla, edible orchid wildflower petals

Supplements: colloidal silver, trace element liquid minerals Etherium Gold (Harmonic Innerprizes)

Exercise: sun salutations, lunar yoga poses, dance, meditation

Recipes: <u>sunlight shake</u>: pineapple, hemp seed, coconut flakes and coconut water, ginger, Etherium gold powder and any Bach remedy or elixir essence you are using for support

Therapies: visualization of golden sun going through body to balance entire system, sunbathing and moon bathing, stargazing, connecting to sound therapy of star rhythms

Aromatherapy: Lilly oil, orchid, jasmine, rose, geranium,

Therapy stone: sunstone – increases vitality, energizes every chakra, alleviates stress and supports whole self

Crown (7th chakra)

Colors to use: soft violet lavender, or white

Location of chakra: just above top center point of skull

Element: illuminated high crystal frequency

Energetic ability: clarcognizance

Protein: hemp seed or powder, sprouted raw flax seeds, raw almonds

Juice: coconut milk or juice, edible rose water, prayer infused spring water

Fruit/Veg: daikon radish, violet grapes, coconut shreds, blackberries,

Herbs: lavender, mint, edible rose petals

Supplements: chamomile, skullcap, Etherium Gold

Exercise: dance, jumping on trampoline or rebounder, high altitude climbing, yoga poses include lotus pose, headstands and pranayama breathing

Recipes: ***pink goddess shake***: banana, organic raspberries, raw coconut, coconut oil, coconut juice, hemp seeds, pomegranate juice, flax seeds (raw sprouted), oat milk, liquid vitex b-12 (B complex from herbs and flowers) few drops of colloidal silver (optional) any Bach remedy. You can use any essence that matches your needs which can be a powerful assistance energetically.

Once blended this creates a light pink shade that reflects the inner lotus within the heart center which can be repeated on a heart center day as well.

Therapies: hair washing (massage your scalp well), swimming in ocean or fresh spring, standing under waterfall, sunbathing, meditation day especially under night sky, tuning forks, toning with singing bowls and all sound therapy

Aromatherapy: Basil (relieves headaches, mental stress, fatigue), violet (insomnia), lavender, rose water/oil tincture (spray over your crown)

Therapy stone: amethyst –psychic protection, helps us unfold to our higher self, balancing to the mind

Third Eye (6th) brow chakra

Color to use: indigo blue

Location of chakra: in between and slightly above eyebrows

Element: telepathic frequency at speed of light

Energetic ability: clairvoyance

Protein: raw cashews, hemp seed, flax seed,

Juice: blueberry, blackberry, plum, red grape, coconut

Fruit/veg: dark red grapes, plums, eggplant, radicchio

Herbs: lemongrass, lavender, chamomile tea, purple basil

Supplements: B complex, omega oils, skullcap, Etherium gold, Etherium black

Exercise: free form dance, facial exercises to massage this ajna point, belly dancing, tai chi, yoga poses include child's pose, seated forward bends

Recipes: same shake base as yesterday with today's fruit variations, fun radicchio and spring green salad with above raw dressing

Therapies: ear candling, acupuncture at ajna point, pancha Karma third eye oil treatment, facial, eye wash, yoga breathing and visualization practice

Aromatherapy: clary sage –(releases mental fatigue),

violet, lemongrass, lavender,

Therapy stone: sodalite – increases self esteem, helps to verbalize truthfulness, directs purpose and self trust

Throat (5th) chakra

Color to use: rich sky blue

Location of chakra: at throat

Element: sound vibration and rhythm

Energetic ability: clairaudience

Protein: hemp seed or powder, flax, coconut (in all forms)

Juice: red grape, blueberry, blackberry, plum, coconut

Fruit/veg: radishes, watercress, daikon, same fruits as juice

Herbs: thyme, blue malva flowers (tea), any lymph draining herbs blessed thistle, ginger, oregano

Supplements: selenium, zinc, magnesium, Etherium black or pink, Aulterra

Exercise: yoga postures to opening the neck (inversions open this center), including camel pose, shoulder stand, bridge pose, gentle stretching in this area

Recipes: blueberry smoothie, edible blue flower petals

Therapies: sound therapy Jonathan Goldman's 'Vocal Toning the Chakras' CD, singing, finger painting, spirited positive debating, shoulder massage, lymph drainage on neck and armpit area.

Aromatherapy: thyme, sandalwood, myrrh

Therapy stone: blue lace agate – gentle assistance in creative expression, grace, activates higher awareness of speech of our self and others

Heart / Inner heart (4th)

Color to use: green – pink (inner heart day 1,6, 30)

Location of the chakra: at heart in center of chest

Element: air

Energetic ability: empathetic caring clairsentience

Protein: super blue green E3 live, spinach, raw pistachio, watercress

Juice: kiwi, green melon, green apple, grapes

Fruit/veg: chives, all greens, kale, sprouts, all green fruits

Herbs: mint, basil, thyme, peppermint

Supplements: vitamin E, omega oils, Etherium Pink, vitamin C

Exercise: any cardiovascular exercise of choice swimming or jogging are excellent choices, yoga poses include cobra, backbends, camel pose

Recipes: spring green salad with fresh sprouted green sun sprouts and fresh avocado and green goddess dressing

Therapies: walking meditation, forgiveness rituals, pranayama breathing, sitting in nature, acupuncture heart points, dry skin brushing, hot cold water therapy to flush circulation throughout system, sacred ceremony to heal

Aromatherapy: essence of lime, pine, rosewood,

thyme, rose, geranium

Therapy stone: aventurine/rose quartz –

aventurine activates, clears and protects the heart, blocks those wanting to hook into our energy

rose quartz spiritually attunes one to higher vibration of love, heals our home environment, opens the inner heart, healing to the inner child

Belly / power (3rd)

Color to use: yellow

Location of the chakra: just above the navel

Element: fire

Energetic ability: level of personal empowerment

Protein: raw cashews, hemp seed, eggs

Juice: pineapple, banana, lemon

Fruit/veg: star fruit, yellow pepper, corn, yellow apple, acorn squash

Herbs: lemongrass, cilantro, ginger, vanilla bean, peppermint, fennel

Supplements: raw maca, raw camu powder, B complex

Exercise: rock climbing, kick boxing, anything building strength can support this center, yoga poses include pit pose, handstands and abdominal strengthening, pranayama fire breath

Recipes: repeat sunshine smoothie from 8th chakra

Therapies: intestinal massage, adrenal support, qui gong or yoga breathing, play in the sun, yellow glasses (color therapy), Bach remedy of Larch (to heal low esteem)

Aromatherapy: lemon, lemongrass, vanilla, geranium, fir, fennel

Therapy stone: citrine – energizes solar plexus, increases endurance, provides greater mental focus, uplifting to mood

Sacral (2nd)

Color to use: bright orange

Loaction of chakra: just below the navel

Element: water

Energetic ability: environment/physical clairsentience

Protein: hemp, raw almonds, walnuts

Juice: peaches, cantaloupe, tangerine, papaya

Fruit/veg: pumpkin, butternut squash, apricots

Herbs/spice: orange zest, cinnamon, nutmeg, cloves, ginger, garlic, orange habanera peppers

Supplements: B vitamins (energy and blood production), probiotics for gut, digestive enzymes, fiber, liquid trace minerals

Exercise: swimming (water element), yoga poses to balance and strengthen abdomen, sit ups, cat cow or locust pose

Recipes: Thai Rainbow nectar soup (recipe above) is excellent (you can add orange shreds of butternut squash or sweet potato if you like)

Therapies: acupuncture to second chakra points, castor oil to belly with heat intestinal massage, colonics series to increase colon strength

Aromatherapy: chamomile, cinnamon –(helping to prevent urinary infections and indigestion)

Therapy stone: carnelian – supports creativity, helps

one to stabilize, aligns one to greater inspiration in life

Base (1st) ground or root chakra

Color to use: red

Location of the chakra: base of spine

Element: earth

Energetic ability: mineral and plant kingdom work

Protein: flax, hemp, most raw nuts

Juice: watermelon, strawberries, cherries, raspberries

Fruit/veg: any root or ground veggie like beet, leek, radishes

Herbs: cinnamon, nutmeg, clove, ginger

Supplements: iron, liquid mineral supplements

Exercise: any outdoor exercise, walking in nature, yoga stretching and body drops to develop stability, ground stretching

Recipes: Warm blanket casserole: 3 cups organic veggie broth with sea salt, crushed garlic, cilantro, to one cup fresh baby orange lentils add when at gentle boil, then turn to low heat and cover for 25-30 min. Add fresh chopped cilantro, scallion, ginger, and Braggs when finished. This nourishes the sacral and base center and brings harmony within.

Therapies: acupuncture at base chakra points, colonics, urinary support herbs, unsweetened

100% unsweetened cranberry juice, ground nap outside, whole body mud or seaweed wrap, potting plants, clay sculpting, uv sauna

Aromatherapy: angelica, cedar wood (grounding) cinnamon, juniper (urinary support)

Therapy stone: red jasper – nurturing to the base, grounding, protective, balances the physical and emotional with the etheric body

Transition day / ground chakra

Color to use: earthy brown, grey or black

Location of chakra: ground below the feet

Element: minerals within earth, connection to core

Energetic ability: core crystal and mineral kingdom work

Protein: flax, hemp, walnuts, raw wheat germ

Juice: coconut water, kale green juice, root veggie juice

Fruit/veg: beets, daikon, coconut, any mineral rich fruit

Herbs: fresh raw cocoa beans, raw cocoa powder, cinnamon, nutmeg, cloves, ginger

Supplements: copper, sea salt, liquid mineral, dulse

Exercise: outside yoga, hiking in forest, snorkeling, digging holes for planting also connects to this underground essence, yoga poses include all inverted poses (to settle and breathe underneath your body), shavasana

Recipe: Earth harmony raw salad: gold or red beet, daikon, cilantro, red apple, field greens, scallion, raw olives, lemon juice and Celtic salt to taste

Therapies: acupuncture request proper draining points to be stimulated, castor oil pack on belly or as guided, mud clay bath

Aromatherapy: anything earthy is great, sandalwood

or any natural wood, or spicy scent

Therapy stone: black tourmaline – provides further grounding and protection, repels negativity

Cathleen Miller is a master intuitive healer and holistic counselor, gifted to translate and harmonize multi-dimensional layers of quantum field information. She is the creator of many conscious life balancing programs and life transforming sacred retreats around the world. She is the owner of Nature Spirit Holistics, in addition to seeing clients in Medical Integrative centers, and top Holistic Resort Spas around the world. To see testimonials and upcoming events go to:

:

www.livingthespiral.com

other titles available by Cathleen Miller

Living Illumination – fire walking

The Lemurian Spectrum – the New Earth alignment

www.ingramcontent.com/pod-product-compliance
Lightning Source LLC
LaVergne TN
LVHW050617100826
845148LV00011B/1624